A SOURCE BOOK
OF
SCOTTISH HISTORY

VOLUME ONE

A SOURCE BOOK
OF
SCOTTISH HISTORY

VOLUME ONE
From Earliest Times to 1424

Edited by

William Croft Dickinson D.Lit., LL.D.

Gordon Donaldson M.A., Ph.D.

Isabel A. Milne M.A.

THOMAS NELSON AND SONS LTD
LONDON EDINBURGH PARIS MELBOURNE
TORONTO AND NEW YORK

THOMAS NELSON AND SONS LTD
Parkside Works Edinburgh 9
3 Henrietta Street London WC2
312 Flinders Street Melbourne C1
5 Parker's Buildings Burg Street Cape Town

THOMAS NELSON AND SONS (CANADA) LTD
91–93 Wellington Street West   Toronto 1

THOMAS NELSON AND SONS
19 East 47th Street New York 17

SOCIÉTÉ FRANÇAISE D'EDITIONS NELSON
25 rue Henri Barbusse Paris Ve

———

First published October 1952

PREFACE

IT has long been apparent that one of the prime needs for the teaching of Scottish history was a work bringing together in convenient form a selection of excerpts from the more important sources upon which that history is based. Such a work would not only encourage pupils and students to ' go to the sources ' and show them what those sources were, but would also provide the teacher with a collection of documents to which he could refer without the necessity of using and quoting a large number of different texts.

The present volume has been produced to meet our own need. It is our hope that it will also meet the needs of others.

Some of those who use the book are bound to feel that other documents and other extracts should have been included, either as additions or as being more suitable to illustrate some aspect of the history of the time. We would gladly welcome suggestions of other documents and extracts from any readers who care to write to us, so that, should a second edition be called for, it may be an improvement upon this first attempt.

This first volume covers the period up to 1424 ; it is our intention to produce a second volume, covering the period from 1424 to 1567, and a final volume, covering the period from 1567 to 1707.

In the task of checking the documents, extracts and translations we have received, and record, much helpful and generous assistance from Miss Barbara Harvey. In the assembling of the documents for the period to 1286 we received the kind co-operation of Dr A. O. Anderson who willingly gave us permission to use a number of extracts from his *Scottish Annals from English Chroniclers* and from his *Early Sources of Scottish History*, and who supplied three corrigenda notes. Dr A. B. Taylor also willingly gave us permission to use one extract from his edition of the Orkneyinga Saga.

W. CROFT DICKINSON
GORDON DONALDSON
ISABEL A. MILNE

EDINBURGH
1952

CONTENTS

ABBREVIATIONS

A.P.S.	Acts of the Parliaments of Scotland
E.R.	The Exchequer Rolls of Scotland
E.S.	*Early Sources of Scottish History,* ed. A. O. Anderson
L.C.	*Early Scottish Charters,* ed. Sir Archibald Lawrie
Nat. MSS Scot.	The National Manuscripts of Scotland
R.M.S.	Register of the Great Seal of Scotland
S.A.	*Scottish Annals from English Chroniclers,* ed. A. O. Anderson
S.H.R.	*Scottish Historical Review*

The sign × between dates indicates 'not earlier than . . . and not later than . . .', e.g. 1124 × 1126 indicates 'not earlier than 1124 and not later than 1126.'

SECTION I

TO 1286

CHAPTER ONE

EARLY DESCRIPTIONS OF SCOTLAND

TACITUS

The Roman historian Tacitus wrote a life of his father-in-law,
Agricola, about A.D. 96. In it he gives a description of Britain
as it was when Agricola became governor there in the year 77.

Britain is the largest of the islands of which the Romans
have knowledge. As to its extent and position—it lies
opposite Germany on the east and Spain on the west,
while in the south it is visible from Gaul ; its northern
shores face no land, but against them beats a vast open
ocean. The shape of the whole of Britain has been likened
by the best writers—Livy among the older and Fabius
Rusticus among the more modern—to an oblong dish or a
battle-axe.[1] That is its shape only if we omit Caledonia,
but the description has been applied to the whole of Britain.
Actually an immense and shapeless extent of land projects
beyond an isthmus and narrows into a sort of wedge.

It was at this time that a Roman fleet first sailed round
the shores of that farthest sea and proved that Britain is
an island. The same expedition discovered and subdued
the previously unknown islands called the Orcades, and
caught sight even of Thule [2] ; so far their orders extended,
and winter was approaching.[3] They report, however, that
the sea there is sluggish and heavy to row in, and is not even

[1] i.e. a *scutula*, a dish shaped like a trapezium, or the head of a battle-axe

[2] A fleet circumnavigating the Orkneys would see Fair Isle and
Foula, and possibly Fitful Head on the mainland of Shetland.

[3] There are variant readings. One is ' . . . Thule, which snow and
winter had hitherto concealed ' ; and another ' . . . Thule, hitherto
approached only by snow and winter.'

3

raised by the winds [1] . . . . I should add one thing : nowhere does the sea hold wider sway, for many tides set in all directions and the sea does not ebb and flow on the shore only, but penetrates and twists far inland and runs in among even the peaks and mountains as if they belong to it. . . .

The red hair and large limbs of the inhabitants of Caledonia point clearly to a German origin.

Tacitus, *Agricola*, x, xi

BEDE

The English historian Bede (673–735) described the position in Britain following the withdrawal of the Roman legions. The passage, with the exception of the description of the firths of Forth and Clyde,[2] was taken by Bede, almost word for word, from Gildas, who wrote in Wales probably before 547.

From that time, the Britons' part of Britain . . . was completely exposed to pillage. . . . It suffered in agony for many years from two exceedingly ferocious nations from across the sea, the Scots from the west-north-west [3] and the Picts from the north. We say that these nations came from beyond the sea not because they were situated outside Britain, but because they were separated from the Britons' part of it by two inlets of the sea which penetrate, in both length and breath, into the land of Britain, one from the eastern ocean and the other from the western, although they cannot quite touch one another. The eastern has in its midst the city Giudi [4]; the western has

[1] These remarks may represent the impression made on strangers by the powerful tideways in and around the islands. It would certainly be ' heavy ' to row against them, while it might seem surprising that when wind and tide were in conjunction the sea was slight.

[2] cf. *S.A.*, 4*n*

[3] *Circio. Circius* was a west-north-west wind.

[4] Commonly believed to have been an island in the Firth of Forth, perhaps Inchkeith ; but it has been suggested that it was on the mainland (cf. *S.A.*, 24–5*n*).

on it, that is, at the right side thereof, the city Alcluith,[1] which in their tongue signifies ' the rock of Cluith,' for it adjoins the river of that name.

Bede, *Hist. Eccl.*, i, xii

DE SITU ALBANIE

From the reference to Andrew, Bishop of Caithness, this description can be dated 1165 × 1184. It is obviously based on earlier accounts, and is composite.

Of the situation of Scotland, which is shaped in the figure of a man ; how it was first divided into seven districts ; by what name it was formerly called, and by whom inhabited.

We read in the histories and chronicles of the ancient Britons, and in the ancient histories and annals of the Scots and Picts, that the district that is now corruptly called Scotia was of old called Albania, after Albanectus, the younger son of Brutus,[2] the first king of the Britons of Greater Britain[3] ; and after a long interval of time it was called Pictavia, from the Picts, who reigned in it for a period of 1,070 years (according to others, 1,360) ; and now it is corruptly called Scotia.[4]

And the Scots have reigned [there] for a period of 315 years, in the year in which King William the Ruddy, brother of Malcolm, that man of honourable life and virtue, has received the kingdom.[5]

[1] Dumbarton

[2] Brutus the Trojan was reputed to be the grandson of Aeneas who, banished from Italy, made his way to Britain where he founded New Troy (London). The legend is to be found in Geoffrey of Monmouth and elsewhere. See T. D. Kendrick, *British Antiquity*.

[3] But for the origin of the name ' Alba ', see Watson, *The Celtic Place-Names of Scotland*, 10–12.

[4] But see Skene, *Celtic Scotland*, i, 1–3.

[5] William ' the Lion ' succeeded Malcolm IV ' the Maiden ' in 1165. This calculation makes the rule of the Scots over the united kingdom of the Picts and Scots date from 850.

This district bears the form and figure of a man. Its chief part, that is to say, the head, is in Argyle, in the western part of Scotland, above the Irish Sea ; and its feet are upon the sea of Norway. And the mountains and deserts of Argyle resemble the head and neck of a man. And his body is the mountain [range] that is called Mound, which extends from the western sea to the eastern sea ; and his arms are the mountains that divide Scotland from Argyle. The right side extends along Moray, and Ross, and Mar, and Buchan ; his legs are the two principal and notable rivers which descend from the mountains named above, that is, the Mound, and which are called the Tay and the Spey : one of them flows to this side of the mountain, and the other beyond it, into the Norwegian sea. Between this man's legs are Angus and Mearns, to this side of the mountain ; and beyond the mountain other lands, between Spey and the mountain.

Now this land was divided anciently by seven brothers into seven parts.[1] Of these the principal is Angus with Mearns, so named after Oengus, the eldest of the brothers. And the second part is Athole and Gowrie. The third part is Strathearn with Monteith. The fourth of the parts is Fife, with Fothreff ; and the fifth part is Mar, with Buchan. The sixth is Moray and Ross. The seventh part is Caithness, to this side of the mountain, and beyond the mountain ; because the mountain of Mound divides Caithness through the middle.[2]

Each of these parts, then, was called a district [3] ; and rightly, because each of them had in it a subordinate district.[4] For this reason were these seven brothers aforesaid regarded as seven kings, because they had beneath them seven under-kings. These seven brothers divided the

[1] The legend of seven sons, or seven brothers, is evidence only of certain early territorial divisions and of their names.

[2] There is here some confusion of the Mound with a more northerly range of mountains, but Skene's suggestion of the Ord of Caithness is hardly acceptable.

[3] regio　　　　　　　[4] subregionem

kingdom of Scotland into seven kingdoms, and each of them in his time reigned in his kingdom.[1]

As a trustworthy narrator has told me—Andrew, a venerable man, bishop of Caithness ; by nation a Scot, and a monk of Dunfermline—the first kingdom [extended] from the excellent piece of water, called in Scottish the *Froch*, in British the *Werid*, and in Roman *Scottewattre*,[2] that is, *Aqua Scottorum* [3] (which [4] divides the kingdoms of Scots and of English, and runs near the town of Stirling) ; as far as to another noble river, called the Tay.

The second kingdom [extended] from the Tay to the *Hilef*,[5] encircling [the first] like the sea, as far as the mountain that is called *Athran*,[6] in the northern part of Stirling. The third kingdom [extended] from the *Hilef* to the Dee. The fourth kingdom [extended] from the Dee to the great and wonderful river that is called the Spey, the greatest and best [river] in all Scotland.

The fifth kingdom [extended] from the Spey to the mountain of Druimm-nAlban.[7]

The sixth kingdom was Moray and Ross.

The seventh kingdom was Argyle.

The name Argyle means the shore of the Scots or the Irish, because all Irish and Scots generally are called Gaels, from one of their primeval leaders, Gaidel Glass. And the Irish used always to land there, to do injury to the Britons. Or for this reason, because the Scots [and]

---

[1] ' A different (and older) account appears in the Chronicle of the Picts, version A (*Chronicles of the Picts and Scots*, 4) : " Cruidne, Cinge's son, the father of the Picts that dwell in this island, reigned for a hundred years. He had seven sons. These are their names : Fib, Fidach, Floclaid, Fortrend, Got, Ce, Circinn." ' (Anderson, *Early Sources*, i, cxvii, *note*.)

[2] [Read, with the MS, *Scottewatre*.—A.O.A.]   [3] The Forth

[4] [For ' which ' (Skene's *que*), read ' because it ' (in MS, *quia*)—A.O.A.]   [5] Probably Glen Isla

[6] According to Skene, Airthrey, about one-and-a-half miles east-south-east of Bridge of Allan

[7] That is, ' the Spine of Britain.' Skene's reading of *Breadalbane* is hardly acceptable.

Picts first dwelt there after their return from Ireland ; or because the Irish occupied these parts in opposition to the Picts ; or because of what is more certain, that that part of the district of Scotland is nearest to the land of Ireland.

E.S., i, cxv–cxix [1]

[1] Anderson's translation from the original Latin in Skene's *Chronicles of the Picts and Scots*, 135–7. See also Skene, *Celtic Scotland*, iii, 42–9, and Chadwick, *Early Scotland*, 34–40.

CHAPTER TWO

THE MAKING OF THE KINGDOM

The land of modern Scotland was at one time held by Picts, Scots, British, Angles and Norse. The Picts held the land roughly north of the Forth and Clyde ; the Scots established themselves in modern Argyll in the fifth and sixth centuries ; the British, holding Strathclyde, were part of the ancient British who had been driven west by invading Angles and Saxons ; the Norse established themselves in Orkney and Shetland, Caithness and Sutherland, and the Western Isles, in the ninth century. The Picts and the Scots were united under Kenneth mac Alpin about 843–50 ; the British kingdom of Strathclyde was joined to the united kingdom of the Picts and Scots with the accession of Duncan I in 1034 ; Lothian (part of the Anglian kingdom of Northumbria) may have been gifted to Kenneth Malcolm's son by Edgar, king of England, and it was certainly secured and held by the battle of Carham (1016 × 1018).

ANGLIAN PRESSURE

In the early years of the seventh century the rapid expansion of the Anglian kingdom in north-east England under King Ethelfrith brought it into conflict with the Scots. The trial of strength between the two peoples at Degsastane is described in the first extract. Although Bede's account of Anglian achievements should be read with a certain caution, it is clear that northward penetration subsequently brought the whole of Lothian within the bounds of the Anglian kingdom and apparently gave it considerable, though obscure, influence over the Pictish kingdom north of the Forth. Further expansion in that direction was, however, resisted, and in 685, at the battle of Dunnichen or Nectan's Mere, the Anglian dominion in the north received a crushing blow. Westwards, the Tyne and the line of the Roman wall provided the Angles with easy access to the Cumbrian coast, so that a wedge was driven between the Britons of Strathclyde and those of Wales and a way lay open for consistent

9

penetration into Dumfriesshire and Galloway. By the eighth century Galloway was regarded as part of Northumbria, and Whithorn was the seat of an Anglian bishopric.

603. In these times Ethelfrid, a most powerful king, and very eager for glory, reigned over the kingdom of the Northumbrians ; and he more than all the princes of the Angles wasted the nation of the Britons so that he seemed comparable with Saul, at one time king of the Israelite nation—with this exception only, that he was ignorant of the divine religion. For no one among tribunes, no one among kings, after expelling or subduing the inhabitants, made more of their lands either tributary to the English nation or habitable by them. . . .

Wherefore Aidan, king of the Scots who dwell in Britain, was disturbed by his advance, and came against him with a huge and mighty army ; but he was conquered, and fled away with few. For almost all his army was slain in a most renowned place which is called Degsastán [1] ; that is Degsa stone. . . .

And never from that time has any of the kings of Scots even to this day dared to come to battle in Britain against the nation of the Angles.

Bede, *Hist. Eccl.*, i, xxxiv (*S.A.*, 11–12)

664. . . . Wilfrid administered the episcopate of the church of York, and also of all the Northumbrians ; but of the Picts also, so far as King Oswy could extend his empire.

Bede, *Hist. Eccl.*, iv, iii (*S.A.*, 36)

681. And Eadhaed, Bosa and Eata were ordained at York by archbishop Theodore ; and he also added two bishops to their number, three years after the departure of Wilfrid —Tunbert to the church of Hexham (Eata remaining at

[1] Generally identified as Dawston in Liddesdale, but Stenton queries this (*Anglo-Saxon England*, p. 77n).

the church of Lindisfarne) and Trumwin to the Pictish province which at that time was subject to the empire of the Angles.

Bede, *Hist. Eccl.*, iv, xii (*S.A.*, 38)

685. For in the next year the same king [Egfrid], who had rashly led an army to ravage the province of the Picts,—although his friends greatly opposed it, and especially Cuthbert of blessed memory who had been recently ordained bishop—was led on by the enemy's feigning flight into the defiles of inaccessible mountains, and was killed along with the chief part of the troops which he had brought with him.[1] . . .

And from this time the hope and valour of the kingdom of the Angles began to ' ebb, recede and sink.' [2] For both the Picts and the Scots who were in Britain recovered the land of their possession which the Angles held ; of the Britons also considerable part recovered their liberty ; and they have it even yet, after about forty-six years.

And there among very many of the English race who were slain by the sword, or given up to slavery, or who escaped by flight from the land of the Picts, the most reverend man of the Lord, Trumwin also, who had received the bishopric over them, retreated with his followers who were in the monastery of Abercorn—placed, it is true, in the district of the Angles, but in the neighbourhood of the firth which separates the lands of Angles and Picts.

Bede, *Hist. Eccl.*, iv, xxvi (*S.A.*, 42–4)

UNION OF THE KINGDOMS OF THE PICTS AND THE SCOTS

The extracts from the *Chronicle of the Kings of Scotland*, recording the death of Kenneth mac Alpin in 858, indicate a conquest of the Picts by the Scots about 843—a conquest which was apparently consolidated about 850. In 900 the *Annals of Ulster* record the death of Donald (Kenneth mac Alpin's grandson) ' King of

---

[1] At Nechtansmere near Forfar   [2] Vergil. *Aeneid*, ii, 169

Alba.' The two kingdoms of the Picts and the Scots have been united to become the ' Kingdom of Alba '—that part of modern Scotland lying to the north of the Clyde and the Forth.

Kenneth mac Alpin may have been related on his mother's side to the Pictish royal house ; but the extracts from the *Annals of the Four Masters* (836) and from the *Annals of Ulster* (839) indicate that the Scots had recently received reinforcements from Ireland, and that, later, the Picts had suffered a heavy defeat by the Danes. These two events may have enabled Kenneth mac Alpin to assert dominion over the Picts. And that is the story related in the *Chronicle of the Canons of Huntingdon*, though that chronicle is a poor authority.

The translations are those of A. O. Anderson in *Early Sources of Scottish History*, i, 255, 267, 268, 271, 288, 289. See also : ibid., i, 268, *note* 3 ; Skene, *Celtic Scotland*, i, 307–10 ; and Chadwick, *Early Scotland*, 21–5.

794. Devastation of all the islands of Britain by the gentiles.

Annals of Ulster, i, 274 (cf. *E.S.*, i, 255)

836. Godfrey, Fergus' son, lord of Oriel,[1] went over to Scotland to reinforce Dalriata, at the bidding of Kenneth, Alpin's son.

Annals of the Four Masters, i, 452 (cf. *E.S.*, i, 267)

839. A battle [was fought] by the gentiles [2] against the men of Fortriu, and in it fell Eoganan, Angus' son,[3] and Bran, Angus' son, and Aed, Boanta's son ; and others fell, almost without number.

Annals of Ulster, i, 342 (cf. *E.S.*, i, 268)

---

[1] The Airgialla of Ireland, associated with Loarn (*E.S.*, i, clii). The district of Oriel in Ireland was immediately to the south-west of Dalriada.

[2] Probably Danes. The chroniclers called both the Danes and the Norse ' gentiles ' ; though sometimes they differentiated between ' black gentiles ' and ' white gentiles.'

[3] Eoganan, son of Angus, was King of the Picts, ?836–39, though he also appears as King of Dalriada, i.e. he may have asserted some temporary authority in Argyll.

843-58. When Danish pirates had occupied the shores, and with the greatest slaughter had destroyed the Picts who defended their land, Kenneth [Alpin's son] passed over into, and turned his arms against, the remaining territories of the Picts ; and after slaying many, drove [the rest] into flight. And so he was the first of the Scots to obtain the monarchy of the whole of Albania, which is now called Scotia ; and he first reigned in it over the Scots.

Chronicles of the Canons of Huntingdon (Skene, *Chronicles of the Picts and Scots*, 209)

843-58. So Kenneth, Alpin's son, first of the Scots, ruled this Pictland prosperously for sixteen years. Pictland was named after the Picts, whom, as we have said, Kenneth destroyed.[1] . . . Two years before he came to Pictland, he had received the kingdom of Dalriata.

Chronicle of the Kings of Scotland (Version A) (Skene, *Chronicles of the Picts and Scots*, 8)

843-58. Kenneth, Alpin's son, reigned over the Scots for sixteen years, after destroying the Picts. . . . [He] led the Scots from Argyll into the land of the Picts with marvellous astuteness.

Chronicle of the Kings of Scotland (Version D) (Skene, *Chronicles of the Picts and Scots*, 151)

SOUTHWARD EXPANSION

(1) *Strathclyde*

From Bede's account [2] it appears that British power made some recovery after the Anglian defeat at Nechtansmere. An opportunity for further recovery occurred when Northumbria crumbled

---

[1] This version contains no previous reference to a ' destruction ' of the Picts. Some account has been omitted which would have thrown further light on Kenneth mac Alpin's acquisition of the kingdom of the Picts.   [2] *Supra*, p. 11

beneath the Danish onslaught in the ninth century, and by the tenth century the kingdom of Strathclyde seems to have extended into Cumberland and Westmoreland. Negotiations between kings were frequently conducted on their boundaries and Athelstan's meeting with the other kings at Eamont in 926 probably indicates that the River Eamont formed the boundary between Athelstan's English kingdom and the British kingdom of Strathclyde.[1]

The secondary Norse invasion from Ireland striking the west coast in the ninth century [2] created confusion, and the political situation placed the king of Scots in a strong position. The remnant of old Northumbria, centred in Bamborough, was weak ; the Danish kingdom of York was directly threatened by the English northward push ; and Strathclyde, like the rest, was weakened by the new Norse invasions. Edmund's grant of Cumbria to the king of Scots in 945 was probably aimed at reducing the impact of the Norse invasions upon the English kingdom, by making the Scots responsible for resisting them. Strathclyde seems to have incurred the enmity of England by assisting the Norse against Edmund, while the king of Scots was in alliance with him. By reducing Strathclyde's power, and giving the Scots a foothold in the south, Edmund's measure considerably increased Scottish influence over Strathclyde. A dynastic connection already existed,[3] and on the death of Owen, king of Strathclyde, in 1018, Malcolm II was able to appoint his son Duncan to the kingship, leaving the way open for the peaceful incorporation of Strathclyde into the larger kingdom. Duncan is ultimately entitled ' King of Picts, Scots and Cumbrians.'

During Macbeth's reign Cumbria was lost to the earldom of Northumbria under Siward, and Malcolm Canmore was impelled to attempt to regain it, challenging the forces of Norman England. The outcome was Rufus's occupation of Carlisle, and the slaying of Malcolm in the following year (1093). By *c.* 1124 a charter of David to Bruce, of the lands of Annandale, recognised the boundary at the Solway.[4]

---

[1] cf. Stenton, *Anglo-Saxon England*, 328

[2] *Infra,* p. 17

[3] One of Kenneth mac Alpin's daughters had married Run, King of Strathclyde.   [4] *Infra,* p. 57

926. And [Athelstan] subjugated all the kings who were in this island : firstly Howel, king of the West Welsh ; and Constantine, king of the Scots, and Owen, king of Gwent,[1] and Aldred, son of Adulf of Bamborough.

And with pledge and with oaths they confirmed peace, in the place which is called Eamot,[2] on the fourth day before the Ides of July.[3]

Anglo-Saxon Chronicle, MS D (cf. *S.A.*, 66)

945. In this year King Edmund harried all Cumbria,[4] and let [5] it all to Malcolm, king of the Scots, on the condition that he be his helper both on sea and on land.

Anglo-Saxon Chronicle, MSS A, B, C, D (cf. *S.A.*, 74)

973. In the year 973, Edgar the peaceful king of the English . . . after sailing round northern Britain [6] with a huge fleet, landed at the city of Chester ; and eight under-kings met him, as he commanded them, and swore that they would stand by him and be faithful to him both on land and on sea : namely Kenneth, king of the Scots ; Malcolm, king of the Cumbrians [7] ; Maccus, king of very many islands ; and other five : Dufnal, Sigfrith, Higuel, Jacob, Ulfkil.

With these one day he entered a boat and, placing them at the oars, he himself took the rudder's helm, and skilfully steered along the course of the river Dee, and sailed from the palace to the monastery of St John the

[1] Monmouthshire   [2] Eamont, Westmoreland

[3] 12 July

[4] Probably northern Cumbria, south of the Solway, though southern Cumbria may have been included in the grant to Malcolm.

[5] The A.S. is *lat*, probably in the sense of ' allowed it to.' The Latin version in the *Chronicle of Melrose* says, ' commendavit ' which has the sense of ' entrusting ' but which was written much later.

[6] cf. *S.A.*, 76 *note* 3

[7] Possibly Malcolm. son of Donald, son of Eogan. Malcolm, Donald's son, king of the Britons of the north, died in 997 (*E.S.*, i, 517).

Baptist, the whole crowd of earls and nobles accompanying him in similar craft.[1]

Chronicle of Melrose (derived from Florence of Worcester ;
cf. *E.S.*, i, 479)

1092. In this year King William with a great army went north to Carlisle, and restored the town and built the castle ; and he drove out Dolfin,[2] who ruled the land there before. And he garrisoned the castle with his vassals ; and thereafter came south hither, and sent thither a great multitude of churlish folk [3] with women and cattle, there to dwell and to till the land.

Anglo-Saxon Chronicle, MS E (cf. *S.A.*, 108)

(2) *Lothian*

The evidence for Edgar's grant of Lothian to Kenneth II is not contemporary but the account rings true. When the Scottish kings held Cumbria, Lothian was heavily outflanked and virtually untenable by English kings. The battle of Carham (1016 × 1018) strengthened an already existing Scottish hold over Lothian. Symeon of Durham's account that the English army at Carham was composed of men from the Tees to the Tweed tallies with the interpretation that Lothian, the land beyond the Tweed, was already in Scottish hands.[4]

971 × 975. And when [Kenneth] had done him homage, king Edgar gave him Lothian ; and with great honour sent him back to his own.

De Primo Saxonum Adventu, in *S.A.*, 77

1018. In the year of the Lord's incarnation 1018, while Cnut controlled the kingdom of the English, a comet appeared for thirty nights to the peoples of Northumbria,

---

[1] There is almost contemporary support for this story in Ælfric's *Life of St Swithin* (written ?996). See *Eng. Hist. Rev.*, xiii, 505-7.

[2] Dolfin, son of Gospatric (*E.S.*, ii, 37)

[3] *Annals of Waverley* reads *multos villanos*.

[4] See Stenton, *Anglo-Saxon England*, 412n

and with dread presage foreshowed the province's future disaster.

For shortly after—that is, after thirty days—while they fought at Carham against an endless host of Scots, the entire people, from the river Tees to the Tweed, with their nobility, almost wholly perished.

Symeon of Durham (S.A., 81)

The Expansion of Alba to the West and North

The saga of Harald the Fairhaired [1] recounts his activities after he had established himself as sole king of Norway at the battle of Hafrsfjordr in 872 or 874. The saga almost certainly confuses two expeditions, one *c.* 874, when Harald established the earldom of Orkney, and another about twenty years later.

Many powerful men of Norway fled as outlaws before King Harold, and sailed into western piracy ; they were in the Orkneys and the Hebrides in the winters, and in the summers they plundered in Norway, and did there great injury to the land. . . . And when the king wearied of this, it happened one summer that King Harold sailed with his army to west beyond the sea. He came first to Shetland, and slew there all the vikings who did not flee thence. Then he sailed south to the Orkneys, and everywhere there cleaned out the vikings. After that, he sailed as far as the Hebrides, and plundered there ; he slew there many vikings. . . . Then he plundered in Scotland, and fought a battle there. And when he came west to Man, they had learned already what warfare King Harold had been making before . . . ; so all the people had fled into Scotland. . . . King Harold when he sailed from the west gave to earl Ronald [2] the Orkneys and Shetland. But Ronald gave both lands immediately to his brother, Sigurd.

E.S., i, 324, 332–4

[1] As written by Snorre Sturlasson in the thirteenth century
[2] Rognvald, earl of Möre in Norway, father of Rolf the Ganger, first duke of Normandy and ancestor of William the Conqueror

During part of the eleventh century the Norse power in Scotland was concentrated in the hands of Thorfinn, earl of Orkney (1014–1064), who, according to the *Orkneyinga Saga*, ' obtained possession of eleven earldoms in Scotland, all the Sudreyar [Hebrides] and a large territory in Ireland.' [1] In 1098 Magnus Barelegs, king of Norway, deprived Thorfinn's sons of the earldom and set his own son in their place, before proceeding on his famous expedition to the western isles. A century later an important stage in the dissolution of the Norse power was reached when the king of Norway appropriated Shetland and the king of Scots conducted operations in Caithness. About the same time a bishopric of Argyll, in the Scottish province, makes its appearance.[2] Scottish penetration continued, and when King Haakon's attempt to restore Norse authority in the west met with a reverse at Largs (1263) the western isles were formally ceded (1266).

1098. *Magnus Barelegs' Expedition*

[*After telling how King Magnus ' plundered and burned' in the Hebrides and on the Scottish and Irish coasts as far south as the Isle of Man, the saga proceeds :*]

He took possession of Anglesey, the most southerly place where former kings of Norway had owned dominion. . . . King Magnus turned back with his army [and] proceeded first to Scotland. Then men went between him and Malcolm,[3] king of the Scots ; and [the kings] made peace between them, to the effect that king Magnus should possess all the islands that lie to the west of Scotland, all between which and the mainland he could go, in a ship with the rudder in place. But when king Magnus came north to Kintyre, he caused [his men] to draw a skiff across the isthmus [4] of Kintyre, and to set the rudder

---

[1] *Orkneyinga Saga*, ed. J. Anderson, 44 ; Taylor's edn. (189), reads ' nine earldoms.' If Thorfinn's mother was a daughter of Malcolm II it may be that he regarded himself as a rival of Duncan, while he allied himself with Macbeth.　　　　[2] Dowden, *Bishops of Scotland*, p. 377

[3] The king at the time was Edgar.

[4] Between East Loch Tarbert and West Loch Tarbert. (Tarbert = *isthmus*)

in place : the king himself sat in the after-deck, and held the helm. And thus he took possession of the land that then lay to the larboard.[1] Kintyre is a great land, and better than the best island in the Hebrides, excepting Man. A narrow isthmus is between it and the mainland of Scotland ; there long-ships are often drawn across.

E.S., ii, 106-13

1195. *King Sverrir of Norway annexes Shetland*

In the latter days of Earl Harald [2] his son-in-law Olaf and John Hallkel's son gathered a band of men from the Orkneys and went east to Norway against King Sverrir [3] ; . . . Many men of good family from the Orkneys threw in their lot with this army. . . . They fought at Florevaag against King Sverrir and were defeated. . . . After that King Sverrir openly treated Earl Harald as an enemy, and said it was his doing that the band of men had been got together. So it came about that Earl Harald sailed from the west, and Bishop Bjarni [4] with him. The earl put himself in King Sverrir's hands and let him settle the affair between them. King Sverrir then took over from Earl Harald all Shetland with its skatts [5] and dues ; and the Orkney earls have not held it since.[6]

Orkneyinga Saga (ed. Taylor), 348 (cf. J. Anderson's edn., 199)

1196. *William ' the Lion ' attacks Earl Harold*

William, king of Scots, collected a large army, and entered Moray to subdue Harold Macmadit [Maddadsson],

---

[1] i.e. to the south of Tarbert, showing that Magnus crossed from east to west. For Bruce's similar exploit, see *infra*, p. 23.

[2] Harald Maddadsson, *c.* 1140-1206

[3] 1184-1217

[4] Bishop of Orkney

[5] Land taxes hitherto uplifted by the earls

[6] Shetland remained separate from the earldom of Orkney until at least 1379.

who had occupied that land. But before the king entered Caithness Harold fled to his ships, refusing to enter into battle against the king. Then the king of Scots sent his army to Thurso, the vill of the aforesaid Harold, and destroyed his castle situated there. And seeing that the king would wholly destroy his land Harold came to the feet of the king and placed himself at his mercy ; chiefly because a storm raged on the sea, and the wind was against him in his wish to go to Orkney island. And he swore to the king that he would bring to him all his enemies when the king should return another time to Moray, and on this condition the king permitted him to hold the half of Caithness ; and the other half of Caithness the king gave to Harold the younger, the grandson of Ronald,[1] formerly earl of Orkney and of Caithness. . . .

Harold the younger received from Swerre Birkbein, king of Norway, permission to claim the half of Orkney, and . . . invaded Orkney. And Harold the elder would not enter battle with him, but leaving Orkney departed to the island of Man ; and there collected a fleet and many men. Likewise did Harold the younger, and went to the island of Man, wishing to meet with Harold the elder ; but before his arrival Harold the elder entered Orkney by another way with his fleet, and slew all whom he found in Orkney. Hearing this, Harold the younger returned to Caithness at Wick and fought with Harold the elder, and in that battle Harold the younger and all his army were slain. . . .

Harold the elder came to the king of Scots . . . and offered the king plenty of gold and of silver to have again Cathania, that is to say, Caithness. And the king replied to him that he would give him that land if he dismissed his wife, the daughter of Malcolm [Macheth][2] and took again his former spouse, the daughter of Duncan, earl of

---

[1] i.e. 'Saint' Rognvald, earl from 1138 to 1158. Harold Maddadsson and Earl Rognvald were second cousins once removed, being descended from Paul and Erlend, sons of Thorfinn (see p. 18).

[2] [In *S.A.*, ' [Macbeth],' erroneously.—A.O.A.]

Fife ; and gave to him as hostage Laurence, his priest, and Honaver, son of Ingemund. But this Harold refused to do. Therefore Ronald, son of Somerled and king of Man, came to William king of Scots and bought Caithness from him, saving the king's yearly revenue.

Roger Hoveden, *Chronica*, iv, 10–12, in *S.A.*, 316

1256. *The Treaty of Perth*

The agreement and final contract for a settlement of the disagreements, complaints, losses, damage and disputes of the isles of Man and the Sudreys and of the rights thereof was made, with the help of divine providence, between magnificent and illustrious princes the lords Magnus IV, by the grace of God illustrious king of Norway, by his solemn envoys . . . compearing there, on one side, and the lord Alexander III by the same grace illustrious king of Scots, personally compearing there with the clergy and greater magnates of his realm, on the other, in this form, viz :

That the same lord Magnus, king of Norway, . . . granted, resigned and quit-claimed, as well petitory as possessory, for himself and his heirs for ever, Man with the rest of the Sudreys and all other islands on the west and south of the Great Haff,[1] with all rights which he and his progenitors had of old therein or he and his heirs may have in future . . . ; the said islands to be held, had and possessed by the said lord Alexander III, king of Scots, and his heirs, with demesne, homages, rents, services and all rights and pertinents of the same, without detention, along with the right of patronage of the bishopric of Man (saving, in all and by all, the right, jurisdiction and liberty of the church of Nidaros,[2] if it have any, in the bishopric of Man) ; and excepting the islands of Orkney and Yhet-

---

[1] Haff = *sea*
[2] The archbishop of Nidaros (Trondheim) was metropolitan of the see of Man and the Isles until 1472.

land,[1] which the said king of Norway has reserved specially to his dominion, with their demesnes, homages and rents, services and all their rights and pertinents within their borders ; in such wise that the men of the said islands which are ceded, resigned and quit-claimed to the said lord king of Scots, as well lesser as greater, shall be subject to the laws and customs of the realm of Scotland and be judged and dealt with according to them henceforth, but for the misdeeds or injuries and damage which they have committed hitherto while they adhered to the said king of Norway they be no wise punished or molested in their heritages in those islands but stand peacefully therein under the lordship of the king of Scots as other free lieges of the said lord king are known to enjoy the most free justice unless they do anything else on account of which they ought to be justly punished according to the approved laws and customs of the realm of Scotland ; if they should wish to remain in the said islands under the lordship of the said lord king of Scots, they may remain in his lordship freely and in peace, but if they desire to retire they may do so, with their goods, lawfully, freely and in full peace ; so that they be not compelled either to remain or to retire contrary to the laws and customs of the realm of Scotland and their own will.

Therefore the foresaid lord Alexander, king of Scots, . . . and his heirs . . . shall give and render for ever to the said king of Norway and his heirs and their assignees within the octave of the nativity of St John the Baptist, in Orkney, that is, in the land of the lord king of Norway, in the church of St Magnus, into the hand of the bishop of Orkney or the bailie of the said lord king of Norway hereto specially deputed by him, or, if the bishop or bailie be not found there, shall deposit in the said church, in the custody of the canons thereof (for the use of the said lord king of Norway)—who shall give to them letters of discharge and of payment—the sum of a hundred merks good

---

[1] The older Norse spelling was Hjaltland

and lawful sterling money to be counted yearly according to the manner and use of the Roman court and the realms of France, England and Scotland ; and also 4,000 merks sterling to be counted in the same way within the next four years at place and term foresaid, namely, 1,000 merks in the octave of the nativity of St John the Baptist in the year of grace 1267, with 100 merks of the foresaid pension, and in the year of grace 1268 at the same place and time 1,000 merks and 100 merks of the foresaid pension [*and likewise for 1269 and 1270, after which the 100 merks of annual only.*] [1]

A.P.S., i, 420 (from the ' Black Book ')

According to the Chronicle of Lanercost, Alexander III appointed bailiffs in Man in 1266 (*E.S.*, ii, 657). For an account of ' The connexion between Scotland and Man,' see Arthur W. Moore, in *S.H.R.*, iii, 393-409.

The treaty of 1266 was ratified by King Robert I and Haakon V in 1312 (*A.P.S.*, i, 101-3). Barbour, in his *Bruce* (xv, 269-96), relates that King Robert led an expedition to the Isles in or about 1316. Proceeding to Tarbert, the king caused his ships to be drawn across the isthmus, and, as the wind was favourable, he had the sails set. The men of the Isles were utterly dismayed, because an ancient prophecy related that whoever should sail over the isthmus should have the dominion of the Isles.

POLITICAL DISUNITY

Long after Scotland was politically united under one king, the underlying disunity of the component parts remained and is occasionally revealed in documents. Heterogeneity was increased by the English and later Anglo-Norman peaceful penetration from the eleventh century onwards. A fairly large Flemish element also settled in Scotland at this time, and contemporary documents show that Flemings were in possession of many tofts

---

[1] According to the Melrose Chronicle (which had reason to be well informed, since a monk of Melrose was one of King Alexander's envoys to Norway), the annual was paid *pro cognicione homagii facti regi Norwagie a dicto Alexandro.*

and tenements in Scottish burghs. Under the aegis of the kings and Anglo-Norman barons, Anglo-Norman customs, laws and institutions became the chief features of government policy. David I sometimes acknowledged the political reality of his time by addressing his charters *omnibus baronibus suis et hominibus et amicis Francis et Anglis*. More frequently, however, the separate identity of the subjects was recognised more fully, e.g.

Malcolmus rex Scottorum episcopis abbatibus comitibus et baronibus justiciariis vicecomitibus prepositis et ministris Francis et Anglicis Scottis et Galwethiensibus.

The following extracts illustrate in detail the disunity in Scotland and the deep conflict between the native subjects and the Anglo-Norman *parvenu* political aristocracy.

1093-94. And then (on the death of Malcolm and Margaret) the Scots chose as king Donald, Malcolm's brother, and drove out all the English who were with king Malcolm before.

When Duncan, king Malcolm's son,[1] who was in king William's court,—inasmuch as his father had formerly given him as a hostage to our king's father, and he had remained here ever since,—heard that all this had so happened, he came to the king and did such fealty as the king would have of him, and so, with consent, went to Scotland with what aid he could get of English and French, and deprived his kinsman Donald of the kingdom, and was received as king.

But afterwards some of the Scots gathered themselves together and slew almost all his followers ; and he himself escaped with few.

Thereafter they were reconciled, on the condition that he should never again introduce English or French into the land.

Anglo-Saxon Chronicle, MS E (*S.A.*, 117–18)

1094. In this year also the Scots deceived and slew Duncan, their king ; and thereafter took to themselves again as king,

---

[1] Son of Malcolm and his first wife, Ingibjorg (cf. *infra*, p. 30)

a second time, his paternal uncle Donald, by whose direction and instigation [Duncan] was betrayed to death.

Anglo-Saxon Chronicle, MS E (*S.A.*, 118)

1097. Also in this same year, soon after St Michael's mass, Edgar Etheling went with an army into Scotland, with king [William's] aid, and in a hard-fought battle won the land, and drove out king Donald ; and in fealty to king William set up there as king his kinsman Edgar, who was the son of king Malcolm and queen Margaret.

Anglo-Saxon Chronicle, MS E (*S.A.*, 119)·

1138.

In 1138 the army with which David I invaded England is described by an English chronicler with emphasis on its varied character.

Now that wicked army was composed of Normans, Germans, English, of Northumbrians and Cumbrians, of [men of] Teviotdale and Lothian, of Picts (who are commonly called Galwegians) and of Scots ; and none might know their number.

Richard of Hexham, *De Gestis Regis Stephani* (*S.A.*, 181)

David I's invasion of England revealed the difference of outlook between the Anglo-Norman knights on whom he relied in his policy of consolidation, and his Scottish subjects. However diverse the native population of Scotland, the gulf between English and Normans and the ' Scots ' was the fundamental political issue of the day. Using the classic convention of the speech before the battle, the English chronicler Ailred of Rievaulx makes Robert Bruce the spokesman for the Anglo-Normans.

' I am here, O King, thy vassal, to give thee now counsel honourable for thee, advantageous for thy kingdom, to the benefit of thy children hereafter. For it is no wise man's part to look to the beginning of things, and not to their result and conclusion ; or for the present alone to lay aside recollection of the past or provision for the future. Against whom dost thou bear arms today and lead this huge army? Against the English truly and the Normans. O king, are not these they with whom thou hast ever found useful counsel, and ready help, and willing obedience besides? Since when, my lord, I ask thee hast thou found such faith in Scots that thou dost with such confidence divest and deprive thyself and thine of the counsel of the English, the help of the Normans, as if the Scots would suffice alone for thee even against the Scots? New to thee is this confidence in Galwegians, attacking with arms today those by whose aid hitherto thou hast ruled the Scots with affection, the Galwegians with terror. Thinkest thou then, O King, that the heavenly Majesty will behold with favouring eyes when thou seekest to destroy those through whom the kingdom was procured for thee and thine, and security in the kingdom? With what forces or by what aid did thy brother Duncan overthrow the army of Donald and recover the kingdom which a tyrant had usurped? Who but our army restored to the kingdom Edgar thy brother, nay, more than brother? Thou thyself, O King, when thou didst demand from thy brother Alexander the part of the kingdom which the same brother [Edgar] had bequeathed to thee [1] at his death didst obtain without bloodshed all that thou wouldst, through the fear of us. Remember when in a past year thou didst beseech for the aid of the English against Malcolm,[2] the heir of his father's hatred and persecution, how joyful, how eager, how willing to help, how ready for the danger came Walter Espec and very many other nobles of the English to meet thee at Carlisle; how many ships they prepared, how they

[1] This refers to David's holding of southern Scotland during Alexander I's reign. Older historians believed that on Edgar's death, the kingdom was divided between Alexander and David. Modern opinion tends to interpret David's earldom as nothing more than a region of Scotland which he held of King Alexander.

[2] Malcolm Macheth, a natural son of Alexander I (cf. *Chronicle of Holyrood*, Scot. Hist. Soc., 129–30)

26

made war, with what forces they made defence ; how they terrified all thy enemies, until they took Malcolm himself, surrendered to them ; taken, they bound him ; and delivered him over bound. So did the fear of us while binding his limbs bind still more the courage of the Scots, and by quenching all hope of success remove the presumption to rebel.

· ' Whatever hatred, therefore, whatever enmity the Scots have against us is because of thee and thine, for whom we have striven so often against them, and have bereft them of the hope of rebellion, and have reduced them in all things to thee and to thy will. Let the Scots laugh therefore, in that thou procurest for them vengeance upon us, since they have naught else to avenge upon us but that we have loved thee and thine, have been loyal to thee and thine ; that with our arms, our shields, even our very bodies we have protected thy life, have preserved the kingdom for thee. . . .'

And [Robert] delayed not, but after the ancestral custom broke the chain of fealty by which he had hitherto been bound to the king, and returned, not without great grief, to his countrymen.

Ailred of Rievaulx, *Relatio de Standardo* (*S.A.*, 193–5)

Robert's *diffidatio* was not, however, permanent. After David had secured his object—a hold in northern England—and had made peace, Anglo-Normans were restored to favour and continued so in the reign of his grandson, William ' the Lion '. The resentment of the Scots also continued. After William ' the Lion's ' capture by the English at Alnwick in 1174 his army was left leaderless.

·1174.

Now there was in the same army a great number of English, for the towns and burghs of the Scottish realm are known to be inhabited by English. On the occasion, therefore, of this opportunity the Scots declared their hatred against them, innate, though masked through fear of the king ; and as many as they fell upon they slew, the rest who could escape fleeing back to the royal castles.

William of Newburgh, *Historia Rerum Anglicarum* (*S.A.*, 256)

But Utred, Fergus's son,[1] and Gilbert his brother, when they heard that their lord the king of Scotland was taken, immediately returned with their Galwegians to their own lands, and at once expelled from Galloway all the bailiffs and guards whom the king of Scotland had set over them ; and all the English and French whom they could seize they slew ; and all the defences and castles which the king of Scotland had established in their land they besieged, captured and destroyed, and slew all whom they took within them.

Benedict of Peterborough, *Gesta Henrici II*, i, 67–8 (*S.A.*, 256)

1212. Since William, king of Scots, who was now of advanced age, was not able to pacify the interior districts of his kingdom disturbed by revolt, he fled to the king of the English and entrusted to his care himself, and his kingdom, and the only son whom he had. And [John] presented [the son], who was commended to him, with the belt of knighthood and set out with an army to those parts ; and sending his men through the interior of the kingdom he seized the leader of the revolt, Cuthred, surnamed MacWilliam, and hanged him on the gallows. He was of the ancient line of Scottish kings [2] ; and, supported by the aid of Scots and Irish, had practised long hostility against the modern kings, now in secret, now openly, as had also his father Donald. For the more recent kings of Scots profess themselves to be rather Frenchmen, both in race and in manners, language and culture ; and after reducing the Scots to utter servitude, they admit only Frenchmen to their friendship and service.

Walter of Coventry, ii, 206 (*S.A.*, 330n)

[1] Fergus, lord of Galloway   [2] See the table printed *infra*, p. 30

CHAPTER THREE

KINGSHIP AND SUCCESSION TO
THE THRONE

From at least the ninth century the succession of the Scottish kingship was collateral, and the table [1] shows the system in detail. Fordun's account of Kenneth II's abolition of this method of succession may represent an early attempt to introduce descent to the heir of line. The table, however, shows that on Kenneth's death the old custom prevailed, and although Duncan I, the descendant of Malcolm II, succeeded his grandfather, Macbeth's later opposition and the slaying of Duncan indicate an attempt to maintain the collateral system of succession, seen also in the successions of Lulach and Malcolm III.

After Malcolm III's death, change and conflict are evident. Donald Bane's claim in 1093 asserted the collateral principle, but he was opposed by Duncan II, son of Malcolm and his first wife, Ingibjorg, on a claim of *hereditary right* or *by inheritance* as the eldest son of the last king. The succession of the younger sons of Malcolm III, Alexander I and David I, satisfied both systems of succession—both being *brothers* and both being *heirs of line*, as neither Edgar nor Alexander I had children.

Under David I the issue had to be clarified, and David, in accordance with his general feudal policy, wished to ensure the succession of his own son Henry according to the feudal system of descent to the heir of line.

During his lifetime Henry was endowed with the substantial territory of Lothian, was associated with his father in government business, recognised as his heir, and finally entitled *rex designatus*. David's policy became more obvious on Henry's death when Malcolm, David's grandson, succeeded immediately to his father's position as heir. By the end of the thirteenth century the feudal law of succession had become so firmly established that the nobles of Scotland were prepared to accept as ruler Margaret of Norway —a girl only four years old.

[1] p. 30

THE RULE OF THE THRONE

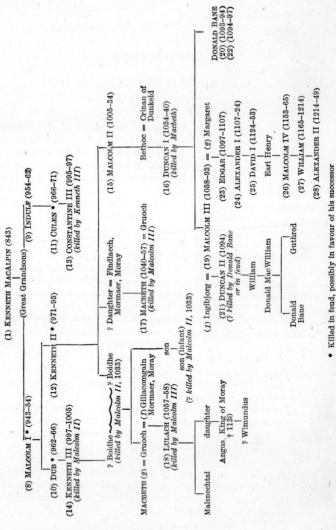

(1) KENNETH MACALPIN (843)

(Great Grandsons)

(8) MALCOLM I * (943-54)

(9) INDULF (954-62)

(10) DUB * (962-66)

(11) CULEN * (966-71)

(12) KENNETH II * (971-95)

(13) CONSTANTINE III (995-97)
(killed by Kenneth III)

(14) KENNETH III (997-1005)
(killed by Malcolm II)

? Boidhe
(killed by Malcolm II, 1033)

? Boidhe

son

son (infant)
(? killed by Malcolm II, 1033)

? Daughter = Findlaech,
Mormaer, Moray

(15) MALCOLM II (1005-34)

Bethoc = Crinan of
Dunkeld

(16) DUNCAN I (1034-40)
(killed by Macbeth)

(17) MACBETH (1040-57) = Gruoch
(killed by Malcolm III)

MACBETH (2) = Gruoch = (1) Gillacomgain
Mormaer, Moray

(18) LULACH (1057-58)
(killed by Malcolm III)

Maelsnechtai

daughter

Angus, King of Moray
† 1130

? Wimundus

(1) Ingibjorg = (19) MALCOLM III (1058-93) = (2) Margaret

(23) EDGAR (1097-1107)

(24) ALEXANDER I (1107-24)

(25) DAVID I (1124-53)

Earl Henry

(26) MALCOLM IV (1153-65)

(27) WILLIAM (1165-1214)

(28) ALEXANDER II (1214-49)

(21) DUNCAN II (1094)
(? killed by Donald Bane
or in feud)

William

Donald MacWilliam

Donald
Bane

Guthred

DONALD BANE
(20) (1093-94)
(22) (1094-97)

* Killed in feud, possibly in favour of his successor

30

King Kenneth [971–95] [1] wished that the law of succession of the ancient kings of his country—who had hitherto reigned in entangled disorder—should be abolished ; and that, after each king, his offspring of legitimate birth should, in preference to the rest, be decked with the kingly diadem. He himself had an illustrious son, named Malcolm; and he proposed to use every endeavour to have the throne assigned to him. He therefore appointed, with the consent of all his chiefs, with the exception of a few supporters of the old rule of succession, that thenceforth every king, on his death, should be succeeded by his son or his daughter, his nephew or his niece ; or by his brother or sister, in the collateral line ; or, in short, by whoever was the nearest survivor in blood to the deceased king, surviving him— even though it were a babe a day old ; for it is said, ' A king's age consists in his subjects' faith ' ; and no law contrary to this has since prevailed.

Fordun, Chronica Gentis Scotorum (edit. Skene), iv, xxix

Now after Malcolm [2] had gained the victory [over Grim[3]], as already described, he did not at once take upon himself the name of king ; but, having summoned together the chiefs of the kingdom, he humbly requested them to give him the crown, if the laws allowed it—not otherwise. They, for their part, fully ratified the law of the royal succession which had been made in his father's days ; and at once appointed him king, crowned with the diadem of the kingdom.

Ibid., iv, xxxix

1094.

Ego Dunecanus, filius regis Malcolumb, constans hereditarie rex Scotiae, dedi in elemosina Sancto Cuthberto et suis servitoribus [4] Tiningeham Aldeham Scuchale Cnolle

---

[1] Kenneth II   [2] Malcolm II

[3] Grim, or Giric, a son of Kenneth III, seems to have ruled over some part of Scotland, under his father. (See *E.S.*, i, 522–3)

[4] i.e. the monks of Durham

Hatheruuich et de Broccesmuthe [1] omne servitium quod
inde habuit Fodanus [2] episcopus : et haec dedi in tali
quitantia cum saca et soca qualem unquam meliorem habuit
Sanctus Cuthbertus ab illis de quibus tenet suas elemosinas.
Et hoc dedi pro me ipso et pro anima patris mei et pro
fratribus meis et pro uxore mea et pro infantibus meis.
Et quum volui quod istud donum stabile esset Sancto
Cuthberto feci quod fratres mei concesserunt. Qui autem
istud voluerit destruere vel ministris Sancti Cuthberti
aliquod inde auferre maledictionem Dei et Sancti Cuthberti
et meam habeat. Amen.

Crux Dunecani Regis X   Scribtoris Grentonis X

Aceard X   Ulf X   Malcolumb X   Eadgari X

Hermer X   Aelfric X   Vinget X

Hemming X   Teodbold X   Earnulf X

L.C., No. xii

Translation

I, Duncan son of King Malcolm, manifest king of Scotland by
inheritance, have given as alms to St Cuthbert and his servants
Tiningeham, Aldeham, Scuchale, Cnolle, Hatheruuich and all
the service from Broccesmuthe which bishop Fothan had from it,
and I have given these things in as good measure with sac and
soc as St Cuthbert ever had most fully from those from whom he
holds his alms. And I have given it for myself and for the soul
of my father, and for my brothers and for my wife and for my
children. And since I wish this gift to be enduring to St Cuthbert
I have obtained the consent of my brothers. Anyone who wishes
to destroy this grant or deprive the servants of St Cuthbert of
anything shall have the curse of God, of St Cuthbert and myself.[3]

[1] Tynninghame, Auldhame, Scoughal, Knowe, Hedderwick, Brox-
mouth

[2] Fothan or Fothad, bishop of the Scots (at St Andrews), d. 1093

[3] This, if genuine, is the earliest extant Scottish charter. It can be
assigned to 1094.

1144 × 1152.

. . . Henricus filius et Deo donante heres meus et Rex designatus. . . .

. . . Henricus gloriosi et illustris Regis David filius et deo propitio heres et rex designatus. . . .

L.C., Nos. clxiii, clxiv

1152. After Pentecost died . . . earl Henry, the son of David, king of Scotland. . . . But King David concealed his grief over the death . . . of his only son, and took forthwith his son's first-born Malcolm,[1] and giving to him as guardian earl Duncan, with a numerous army, commanded that this boy should be conducted round the provinces of Scotland, and proclaimed to be the heir to the kingdom.

John of Hexham, *Historia Regum* (*S.A.*, 227-8)

1284. *At Scone*

To all Christ's faithful to whom this writ shall come, Alexander Comyn, Earl of Buchan, constable and justiciar of Scotland, Patrick Earl of Dunbar, Malise Earl of Strathearn, Malcolm Earl of Lennox, Robert de Bruce, Earl of Carrick, Donald Earl of Mar, Gilbert Earl of Angus, Walter Earl of Menteith, William Earl of Ross, William Earl of Sutherland, Magnus Earl of Orkney, Duncan Earl of Fife, John Earl of Athole, Robert de Bruce, father, James, Steward of Scotland, John de Balliol, John Comyn, William de Soulis, then justiciar of Lothian, Ingerram de Gynis, William de Moray, son of Walter de Moray, knights, Alexander de Balliol, Reginald le Chen, father, William de Sancto Claro, Richard Syward, William de Brechin, Nicholas de Hay, Henry de Graham, Ingerram de Balliol, Alan son of the Earl, Reginald le Chen, son, J. [ ] de Lindesey, Patrick de Graham, [tus] de Maxwell, Simon Fraser, Alexander de Argyle, Angus son of Donald

---

[1] Malcolm IV

33

and Alan son of Roderick, barons of the realm of Scotland, greeting in the Lord.

Know ye that, since it has pleased the Most High that our lord Alexander eldest son of [king] Alexander has gone the way of all flesh with no legitimate offspring surviving directly from the body of the said king, we bind ourselves and our heirs completely by this document to our lord king and the heirs descended from his body directly or indirectly who by right ought to be admitted to the succession and in the faith and fealty by which we are bound to them we firmly and faithfully promise that if our said lord king happens to end his last day in this life leaving no legitimate son or sons, daughter or daughters of his body or of the body of the said Alexander his son, we each and all of us will accept the illustrious girl Margaret, daughter of our lord king's daughter Margaret, of good memory, late queen of Norway, begotten of the lord Eric, illustrious king of Norway, and legitimate offspring descended from her, as our lady and right heir of our said lord king of Scotland, of the whole realm of Scotland, of the Isle of Man and of all other islands belonging to the said kingdom of Scotland, and also of Tyndale and Penrith with all other rights and liberties belonging or of right belonging to the said lord king of Scotland . . . and against all men . . . we shall maintain, sustain and defend [her] with all our strength and power.

A.P.S., i, 424 (from the original deed)

CHAPTER FOUR

THE CHURCH

THE MISSION OF NINIAN

The literary evidence for Ninian consists of (*a*) Bede's eighth-century account of an old tradition ; (*b*) an eighth-century poem on the Miracles of Ninian [1] ; and (*c*) a twelfth-century ' Life,' by Ailred of Rievaulx, who claimed to have used an older book on the life and miracles of Ninian. Archaeological evidence is conclusive that Christianity reached the Galloway area at a very early date, and recent excavations at Whithorn have revealed a church of exceptional antiquity which may actually be the original *Candida Casa*.[2] Thus, although Ninian himself remains a shadowy figure, and much is still controversial, the tradition recorded by Bede and printed below contains nothing improbable.

[*After referring to Columba's mission to the northern Picts, who are separated from the southern by rugged mountains, the narrative proceeds :*]
The southern Picts, who have their seats to this side of the same mountains, had, as they relate, a long time before forsaken the error of idolatry and received the faith of truth, when the word was preached to them by Ninian, a most reverend bishop and very holy man of the race of the Britons who had been regularly trained at Rome in the faith and the mysteries of the truth. And even now [*c.* 730] the English nation holds the see of his bishopric, notable for the name and church of the bishop St Martin ; and there also he rests in the body, along with very many saints. And this place, pertaining to the province of the Bernicians, is commonly called *Ad Candidam Casam*, because

[1] See *Antiquity*, xiv (1940), 280–91
[2] Dumfriesshire and Galloway Natural History and Antiquarian Society, *Transactions*, 3rd Series, xxvii, especially 118–19.

he made there a church of stone, after a custom strange to the Britons.

Bede, *Hist. Eccl.*, iii, 4

THE WORK OF COLUMBA

It seems likely that Christianity spread from Whithorn throughout the south-west of Scotland in the fifth century, and in the sixth century the Strathclyde area was traditionally the scene of the labours of Kentigern, a dim figure about whom there is no evidence earlier than two twelfth-century ' lives.' [1] How far there may have been extension from the south-west to the centre of Scotland and up the east coast remains controversial.

For the work of Columba, in the west, we have the *Life* by Adamnan, written not more than a century after Columba's death. It is not a biography, and is concerned mainly with the miracles and prophecies of the saint, but Columba emerges from it as a real figure. The first extract given below describes Columba's first visit to Brude, king of the Picts, at his fortress probably near Inverness ; the second throws some light on the sacramental doctrine and practice of the Celtic clergy and on their church order. Jurisdiction belonged to the abbot (who might, like Columba, be only a presbyter), yet it is plain that, in order, the episcopate was superior to the priesthood.

At another time, that is, on the Saint's first laborious journey to king Brude, it happened that the king, swollen by royal pride, acted arrogantly, and did not open his castle gates upon the blessed man's first arrival. As soon as the man of God saw this he went with his comrades to the openings of the gates, and, first pressing on them an image of the Lord's cross, then laid his hand upon them, striking against the gates ; and immediately, of their own accord, the bolts were forcibly withdrawn, and the gates opened with all speed. And immediately after they were opened, the saint entered with his companions. Learning this, the king and his council were much afraid ; and he left the house, and

[1] *E.S.*, i, lxxiv-lxxv

went to meet the blessed man with reverence, and addressed him mildly with peaceful words ; and thenceforth from that day all the days of his life the same ruler honoured the holy and venerable man befittingly with very high esteem.

Adamnan, ii, xxxv (cf. E.S., i, 49–50)

A certain disciple . . . came to the Saint, and in humility he disguised himself as much as he could, so that no one might know that he was a bishop ; but yet this could not be hidden from the Saint. For the next Lord's Day, being bidden by the Saint to consecrate the Body of Christ according to custom, he calls the Saint so that, as two priests, they may break the Lord's Bread together. The Saint thereupon, going up to the altar, suddenly looking on his face thus addresses him : ' Christ bless thee, Brother, break this bread alone with the episcopal rite, now we know that thou art a bishop. Why hast thou hitherto tried to disguise thyself that the veneration due to thee by us might not be rendered ? '

Adamnan, i, xliv

THE ACCEPTANCE OF ROMAN USES

Columban Christianity extended into the north of England when King Oswald of Northumbria in 635 obtained from Iona the services of Aidan as abbot-bishop of Lindisfarne. Meantime, from southern England, where Augustine had landed in the year of Columba's death, a church in close fellowship with Rome was advancing northwards. The Celtic and Roman parties clashed in Northumbria, where a decision was made in favour of the latter at the so-called Synod of Whitby in 664.

In these times a great and frequent dispute arose about the observance of Easter, those who had come from Kent or from France protesting that the Scots celebrated Easter Sunday contrarily to the custom of the universal church. . . . The question being raised . . . concerning Easter and the tonsure and other ecclesiastical matters, it was decided

37

that a synod must be held in the monastery which is called
Streaneshalch [i.e. Whitby].

Bede, iii, 25 (*S.A.*, 29, 31)

In the days of Colman, metropolitan bishop of the city of
York,[1] and in the reign of Oswiu [2] and Alchfrid his son,[3] the
abbots and priests and all ranks of the church came together
in the monastery which is called Streuneshalgh. There were
present the most holy Abbess Hilda ; the kings : two
bishops, Colman and Aegilberht ; and they enquired what
was the most correct time for keeping Easter. . . . [*Colman
spoke on the Celtic side*, *Wilfrid on the Roman.*]

Then, when St Wilfrid the priest had ended, King
Oswiu, with a smile, asked them all : ' Tell me, which is
greater in the kingdom of heaven, Columba or the Apostle
Peter ? ' And the whole Synod replied, with one voice
and consent : ' That the Lord decided, when he said,
" Thou art Peter, and upon this rock I will build my
church, and the gates of hell shall not prevail against it.
And I will give unto thee the keys of the kingdom of heaven,
and whatsoever thou shalt bind on earth, shall be bound in
heaven, and whatsoever thou shalt loose on earth, shall be
loosed in heaven." ' The king made answer wisely :
' He keeps the gate and holds the keys ; I make no
controversy with him, nor do I accord with those who
make it, and in my life I will in nothing contradict his
judgments.'

Eddi, *Vita Wilfridi Episcopi* (in Raine, *Historians of the Church
of York*, i, 14–16)

Bede, writing some seventy years after the triumph of Rome at
Whitby, pays the following remarkable tribute to the clergy of the
Celtic church—

---

[1] Colman was bishop of Lindisfarne. Here his biographer reads
into the seventh century the institutions of a later age.

[2] King of Bernicia, 642–70, and of Northumbria, 654–70

[3] Sub-king in Deira, *c.* 654–64

And of how great frugality and of what continence were Colman and his predecessors, even the place [1] which they ruled bore testimony. For when they departed very few houses were found there, excepting the church ; that is, those only without which social intercourse could not exist at all. Apart from flocks they had no moneys. For if they received any money from the rich, they gave it straightway to the poor. For it was not necessary either that moneys should be gathered or that houses should be provided for the entertainment of the powerful of the world, since they never came to church except only for the sake of prayer or of hearing God's word. The king himself, when occasion required, came with only five or six attendants ; and departed when his prayer in the church was ended. And if perchance it happened that they were refreshed there, they were content with only the simple and daily food of the brethren, and asked for nothing more.

For then the whole anxiety of those teachers was to serve God, not the world ; their whole care to cherish their hearts, not their stomachs. And hence also the habit of religion was at that time in great veneration ; insomuch that wherever any cleric or monk arrived, he was joyfully received as a servant of God by all. Yea, if he were discovered as he went upon the way, they ran to him, and, bowing their necks, rejoiced to be either signed by his hand or blessed by his mouth. And they diligently offered a hearing also to their exhortatory words. But on Sundays they flocked emulously to the church or to the monasteries, for the sake not of refreshing the body, but of hearing discourse of God. And if any of the priests chanced to come into a village, straightway the villagers gathered together and endeavoured to learn of him the word of life. For the priests or clerks had themselves no other reason for visiting the villages than to preach, to baptise, and to visit the sick ; and, to speak briefly, to care for souls. For they were to such extent chastened from all taint of avarice

---

[1] Lindisfarne

that none received territories or possessions for the construction of monasteries, unless compelled by the authorities of the world. And this custom was preserved in all things for some considerable time afterwards in the churches of the Northumbrians.

Bede, iii, 26 (S.A., 33-4)

The decision made at Whitby soon made its influence felt north of the Forth, where, early in the eighth century, Nechtan, king of the Picts, decided to adopt the Roman reckoning of Easter. A reference in the *Annals of Tigernach*, s.a. 717, to the ' expulsion of the community of Iona across the ridge of Britain by King Nechtan '[1] suggests that clergy who refused to conform were driven from the Pictish dominions.

? 710.

At this time [2] Nechtan, king of the Picts who inhabit the northern parts of Britain, warned by frequent study of the ecclesiastic writings, renounced the error by which he and his nation had been held hitherto in the observance of Easter, and persuaded himself and all his subjects to celebrate the catholic time of the Lord's resurrection.

And to accomplish this the more easily and with the greater authority he sought aid of the nation of the Angles, whom he knew to have long ago established their religion after the example of the holy Roman and apostolic church. For he sent messengers to the venerable man Ceolfrid, abbot of the monastery of the blessed apostles Peter and Paul, at the mouth of the river Wear and near the river Tyne in the place which is called Jarrow, which he ruled most gloriously . . . requesting him to send him exhortatory letters, with which the more effectively he might be able to confute those who presumed to observe Easter not at its time ; as also concerning the manner or fashion of the tonsure with which it was fitting that clerics should be marked out : excepting that he was himself also to no small extent skilled in these matters.

[1] E.S., i, 217   [2] Probably about 710

And he also asked that architects should be sent to him, to make a church of stone among his people after the manner of the Romans, promising to dedicate it in honour of the blessed prince of the apostles, and also that he himself and all his subjects would always imitate the custom of the holy Roman and apostolic church ; in so far at least as they had been able to learn it, being so far separated from the speech and race of the Romans.

And favouring his pious vows and prayers the most reverend abbot Ceolfrid sent the architects for whom he was asked, and sent to him also a letter. . . .

When this letter had been read in presence of king Nechtan and of many very learned men, and had been diligently interpreted by those who were able to understand it into his own tongue, he is said to have rejoiced greatly in its exhortation ; insomuch that he rose up from the midst of the assembly of his nobles, and bowed his knees to the ground, giving thanks to God that he should be worthy to receive such a gift from the land of the Angles. . . .

'And I profess openly,' [he said,] 'and protest to you present who sit here that I will ever observe, with my whole nation, this time of Easter ; and decree that all clerics who are in my realm must receive this tonsure, which we have heard to be wholly reasonable.' And without delay he fulfilled by his royal authority what he had said. For immediately by public command the nineteen-year cycles of Easter were sent throughout all the provinces of the Picts to be transcribed, learned and observed ; the faulty cycles of eighty-four years being everywhere suppressed. All servants of the altar and monks were tonsured in the manner of the crown ; and the nation corrected rejoiced that it had been devoted as it were to a new discipleship of Peter, the most blessed prince of the apostles, and placed under the protection of his patronage.

Bede, v, 21 (*S.A.*, 47)

THE CHURCH FROM THE EIGHTH TO THE ELEVENTH CENTURY

However far Scotland may have advanced in the eighth century towards conformity with the West European church as a whole, the attacks and settlements of the pagan Norsemen during the next two centuries had the effect of isolating Scotland from Christian Europe, from Ireland and to some extent even from England, with the result that the Scottish church retained, or developed, certain peculiarities in worship and discipline. Scotland escaped the monastic reforms of the tenth and eleventh centuries, and the great ecclesiastical centres continued to be served by Culdees. The initiation of the process of assimilating Scottish ecclesiastical organisation and usages to those of England and continental countries is usually attributed to Queen Margaret. Margaret, however, initiated no reforms in the administration or organisation of the church. She concerned herself only with relatively trivial matters—whether Lent should begin on Ash Wednesday or on the Monday following ; abstinence from labour on the Lord's Day ; the legality of marriage with a stepmother or a deceased brother's widow ; ' barbarous ' rites in the celebration of mass ; and Scottish scruples about unworthy reception of the Holy Communion.[1] There are no indications that Margaret attempted to tackle any of the graver problems, such as the question of clerical celibacy or the dispossession of lay holders of church property. Nor—apart from bringing Benedictines to Dunfermline—did she endow and foster new institutions in the way her sons were to do. Not only so, but in her reign the royal patronage of the Culdees continued, as shown by the following extracts narrating grants to the community of Lochleven.

For prayers and intercessions, Machbet son of Finlach and Gruoch daughter of Bodhe, king and queen of the Scots, granted to Almighty God, and to the Culdees of the island of Lochleven, Kyrkeness with its boundaries . . . [1040 × 1057]

L.C., No. v

[1] E.S., ii, 70–4

Maldunus, bishop of St Andrews, granted the church of Markinch with all its land, honourably and devoutly, to God and St Serf and the Culdees of the island of Lochleven. [*ante* 1055]

L.C., No. vi

King Malcolm and Queen Margaret of Scotland devoutly granted the township of Ballecristin to Almighty God and the Culdees of Lochleven, with the same liberty as previously. [1070 × 1093]

L.C., No. viii

ESTABLISHMENT OF THE DIOCESAN SYSTEM

The position of the Scottish bishoprics *c.* 1100 is very obscure. There had been in earlier times bishops at Glasgow, Abercorn, Whithorn, Abernethy, Dunkeld and St Andrews, and more recently there had probably been one at Mortlach. Certainly some of these sees, possibly others, had lapsed for longer or shorter periods, and even St Andrews was vacant from 1093 until 1109 and again from 1115 to 1120 and 1121 to 1127. In the third and fourth decades of the twelfth century, when evidence suddenly becomes more ample, we find bishops in some seven sees (see the first extract below) and by the middle of the century the entire country had plainly been divided into dioceses. While such a complete *diocesan system* was certainly a novelty, it is for the following reasons rash to assume that the foundation of *episcopal seats* can be definitely assigned to the reigns of Alexander I and David : (1) The bishops' seats were mostly at sites which are known to have been ancient ecclesiastical centres and which were at this time the homes of Culdee communities ; (2) the irregular boundaries of some of the dioceses, especially Dunkeld, Brechin and St Andrews, suggest strongly that an older structure of some kind influenced the system now established [1] ; (3) the account of the restoration of the see of Glasgow (1109 × 1114) indicates

[1] See map of the dioceses in Dunbar's *Scottish Kings*, Skene's *Celtic Scotland*, ii, MacEwen's *History of the Church in Scotland*, i, and the Ordnance Survey's *Map of Monastic Britain* (North Sheet).

that this bishopric had simply suffered from a long vacancy, in much the same way as St Andrews ; (4) there is an inquest into the possessions of the church of Glasgow, of date *c.* 1120, which shows that this see had ancient endowments scattered throughout the diocese [1] ; and (5) in many cases, as the first extract given below shows, the earliest recorded bishop was a Celt and may be the last of an old, and not the first of a new, succession.

1128.

The Scottish Episcopate

[*To the charter of King David to Dunfermline* :] Ego Robertus Sancti Andreae episcopus confirmo. Ego Johannes Glasguensis episcopus confirmo. Ego Cormaccus Dunkeldensis episcopus confirmo. Ego Gregorius Moraviensis episcopus confirmo. Ego Macbeth Rosmarkensis episcopus confirmo.[2]

L.C., No. lxxiv

1109 × 1114.

Restoration of the See of Glasgow

Thomas [archbishop of York] ordained as bishop to the church of Glasgow a holy man, Michael, who gave written profession of canonical obedience to the church of York and to Archbishop Thomas and his successors. . . . Kinsi, archbishop of York [1055–60], had consecrated his predecessors Magsuea and John. . . . But because of hostile invasion and desolation and the barbarity of the land for long the church was without a pastor, until earl David (afterwards king of Scotland) appointed as bishop Michael aforesaid, and sent him over to be consecrated by Archbishop Thomas.

S.A., 133–4

---

[1] *Registrum Episcopatus Glasguensis*, i, 1
[2] Gilla-aldan, bishop of Galloway, appears *c.* 1128 (*S.A.*, 159), and Nectan, bishop of Aberdeen, in 1131–2 (*L.C.*, No. xcvii).

EPISCOPAL ELECTIONS : ERECTION OF CHAPTERS : SUPERSESSION OF THE CULDEES

The traditional method of episcopal appointment was choice by the clergy and people of the diocese with the approval of the king, but in the twelfth and thirteenth centuries this gave way to the election of bishops by cathedral chapters. In most of the Scottish dioceses a chapter consisting of secular clergy was organised, but St Andrews and Whithorn had chapters of canons regular. The first document shows the pope, in 1147, giving to the Augustinian priory of St Andrews (founded in 1144) the right of electing the bishop, and providing that on the deaths of Culdees canons regular should take their places ; and the second (*c.* 1150) shows the similar provision made by King David. To the Culdees of Lochleven, as the third document shows, David about the same time offered a choice of either accepting the Augustinian rule as canons or being expelled from the island.

The developments envisaged in the first and second documents were not realised, for the Culdees of St Andrews were instead transformed into the collegiate church of St Mary of the Rock and, so transformed, claimed at least a share in episcopal elections until the middle of the thirteenth century. The other Culdees throughout the country were either transformed into, or super-seded by, cathedral chapters of secular canons or priories of Augustinian canons regular.

Eugenius . . . to Robert, prior of the church of St Andrew . . . and his brethren. . . . We take the foresaid church . . . under St Peter's protection and ours . . ., ordaining that the canons' order (according to the rule of St Augustine) which is known to be established in that church by the grace of God, the counsel and aid of our venerable brother Robert, our bishop, and your own toil and attention, should be preserved inviolably there in all time coming. . . .

On the death of our brother, Robert, your bishop, no one shall be promoted in the church of St Andrews, which is an episcopal see, by any underhand device or by violence, but only one who is thought fit to be chosen, canonically and under God, by you, in common consent, or by the portion of the brethren of your church of sounder counsel.

We also provide that on the death of Culdees, canons regular shall, under God, be substituted in their place.

L.C., No. clxxxi

David, king of Scots, to his bishops, abbots, earls, sheriffs and all sons of holy church, greeting. Know that I have given and granted to the prior and canons of the church of St Andrew the apostle that they may receive the Culdees of Kilrimont [1] as canons among them with all their possessions and revenues if they wish to become canons, and if they do not wish to become canons those who are now alive shall have and hold their possessions for their lives, and after their deaths there shall be appointed in their place as many canons in the church of St Andrews as there are Culdees so that all their wealth, their lands and alms which they have, may be converted to the use of the canons of the aforesaid church in as perpetual and free alms as any church holds in my kingdom.

L.C., No. ccxxxiii

David, king of Scots, to his bishops, abbots, earls, sheriffs and all honest men of all his land, greeting. Know that I have granted and given to the canons of St Andrew the island of Lochleven in order that they may there institute an order of canons, and that any of the Culdees who are found there, who are willing to live according to the rule, shall remain there in peace with them and under them, but if any wish to resist this, I wish and command that they be expelled from the island.

L.C., No. ccxxxii

[1] i.e. St Andrews

THE DEVELOPMENT OF THE PARISHES AND THEIR APPROPRIATION TO MONASTIC HOUSES

The following charter is usually considered to be the earliest reference to the endowment of a parish church. Its significance is twofold : it illustrates the process whereby a landowner built a church and endowed it with a ploughgate of land ; but it also shows that the church, so far from becoming an independent parish church served by its parson, was at once handed over to the monks of Durham. The ' appropriation ' of parish churches to religious houses is further illustrated in the foundation charter of Holyrood.

c. 1105. *Charter by Thor Longus to the Monks of Durham*

Omnibus sanctae matris ecclesiae filiis, Thor longus in Domino salutem. Sciatis quod Aedgarus, dominus meus, rex Scottorum, dedit mihi Aednaham desertam quam ego suo auxilio et mea propria pecunia inhabitavi, et ecclesiam in honorem Sancti Cuthberti fabricavi, quam ecclesiam cum una carrucata terrae Deo et Sancto Cuthberto et monachis ejus in perpetuum possidendam dedi. Hanc igitur donationem feci pro anima domini mei, regis Aedgari, et pro animabus patris et matris illius et pro salute fratrum et sororum ipsius et pro redemptione Leswini, fratris mei dilectissimi, et pro meimet ipsi tam corporis quam animae salute. Et si quis hanc meam donationem Sancto praedicto et monachis sibi servientibus aliqua vi vel ingenio auferre praesumpserit, auferat ab eo Deus Omnipotens vitam regni coelestis et cum diabolo et angelis ejus poenas sustineat aeternas : Amen.

L.C., No. xxiv, cf. ibid., No. xxxiii

[Thor the Long relates that King Edgar gave him Ednam, which was waste but which he occupied and cultivated ; that he built a church in honour of St Cuthbert, and that he gave it, with a ploughgate of land, to the monks of Durham.]

1127. *Some Scottish Parish Priests*

[*Witnesses to a grant by Robert, bishop of St Andrews, to the church of Coldingham, made at Roxburgh on 17 July 1127 :*]

Robert, clerk, brother of the same bishop ; Blahan, priest of Linton [1] ; Adulf, priest of Aldehamstoc [2] ; Henry, priest of Lienhall [3] ; Orm, priest of Houm [4] ; Osbern, priest of Ednam ; John, priest of Legerwood. . . .

S.A., 164 ; cf. *L.C.*, No. lxxiii

1128 × 1136.

The Foundation Charter of the Abbey of Holyrood

In the name of our Lord Jesus Christ, and in honour of the Holy Rood, and of Saint Mary the Virgin, and of all the Saints, I, David, by the grace of God king of Scots, of my royal authority, and with the assent of Henry my son and the bishops of my kingdom, and with the confirmation and testimony of the earls and barons, the clergy and the people also assenting, of divine prompting, grant all the things underwritten to the Church of the Holy Rood of Edinburgh, and in perpetual peace confirm them. These therefore are what we grant to the aforesaid Church and to the canons regular serving God therein in free and perpetual alms. To wit, the Church of the Castle with all its appendages and rights. And the trial of battle, water, and hot iron, as far as belongs to ecclesiastical dignity ; and with Salectun [5] by its right marches ; and the Church of Saint Cuthbert, with the parish and all things that pertain to that church, and with the Kirkton by its right marches, and with the land in which that Church is situate ; and with another land that lies under the Castle, to wit, from the spring that rises near the corner of my garden, by the road that leads to the Church of Saint Cuthbert, and on the other side under the Castle until you come to a crag which is under the Castle towards the east ; and

[1] East Linton   [2] Oldhamstocks   [3] Coldstream
[4] Home   [5] Saughton

with the two chapels which pertain to the same Church of Saint Cuthbert, to wit Crostorfin [1] with two oxgates and six acres of land, and that chapel of Libertun with two oxgates of land, and with all the tithes and rights, as well of the living as of the dead, of Legbernard,[2] which Macbetber gave to that Church, and which I have granted ; And the Church of Hereth [3] with the land that belongs to that Church, and with all the land that I have added and given to it, as my servants and good men walked its bounds and gave it over to Alwin the Abbot, with one salt-pan in Hereth, and twenty-six acres of land. Which Church and land aforenamed, I will that the canons of the Holy Rood hold and possess for ever freely and quietly ; and I strictly forbid that any one unjustly oppress or trouble the canons or their men who live in that land, or unjustly exact from them any works or aids, or secular customs. I will moreover that the same canons have liberty of making a mill in that land, and that they have in Hereth all those customs, rights and easements, to wit in waters and fishings, in meadows and pastures, and in all other necessary things, as they best held them on the day in which I had it in my domain ; And Broctun [4] with its right marches ; and Inverlet, that which is nearest the harbour, with its right marches, and with that harbour, and with the half of the fishing, and with a tithe of the whole fishing which belongs to the Church of Saint Cuthbert ; And Petendrei,[5] with its right marches ; and Hamere [6] and Ford, with their right marches ; and the hospital, with one plough of land ; And forty shillings from my burgh of Edinburgh yearly ; and a rent of a hundred shillings yearly for the clothing of the canons, from my cain of Perth, and this from the first ships that come to Perth for the sake of trade ; and if it happen that they do not come, I grant to the aforesaid Church, from my rent of Edinburgh forty shillings, and from Stirling twenty shillings, and from Perth forty shillings ;

[1] Corstorphine   [2] Leadburn   [3] Airth   [4] Broughton
[5] Pittendreich, near Lasswade   [6] Whitekirk

And one toft in Stirling, and the draught of one net for fishing ; and one toft in my burgh of Edinburgh free and quit of all custom and exaction ; And one toft in Berwick, and the draught of two nets in Scypwell ; and one toft in Renfrew of five roods, and the draught of one net for salmon, and to fish there for herrings freely ; And I forbid that any one exact from you or from your men, any customs therefor. I grant moreover to the aforesaid canons from my chamber yearly, ten pounds to the lights of the Church, and to the works of that Church, and to repairing these works for ever. I charge, moreover, all my servants and foresters of Stirlingshire and of Clackmannan, that the Abbot and Convent have free power in all my woods and forests, of taking as much timber as they please and wish for the building of their church and of their houses, and for any purpose of theirs. And I enjoin that their men who take timber for their purposes in the said woods, have my firm peace, and so that ye do not permit them to be disturbed in any way ; And the swine the property of the aforesaid Church, I grant in all my woods, to be quit of pannage. I grant moreover to the aforesaid canons the half of the fat, tallow and hides of the slaughter of Edinburgh and a tithe of all the whales and sea-beasts which fall to me from Avin to Colbrandespade [1] ; And a tithe of all my pleas and gains from Avin to Colbrandespade ; And the half of my tithe of my cain, and of my pleas and gains of Kentyr and Argyll, and all the skins of rams, ewes, and lambs of the Castle and of Linlitcu which die of my flock ; And eight chalders of malt, and eight of meal, and thirty cart loads from the bush of Libertun ; And one of my mills of Dene, and a tithe of the mills of Libertun and Dene, and of the new mill of Edinburgh, And of Craggenemarf, as much as I have in my domain, and as much as Viueth the White gave them in alms of the same Crag.[2] . . . I

[1] From the River Avon to Cockburnspath

[2] The clause, permitting the establishment of a burgh, omitted here, is printed *infra*, p. 70.

grant moreover that the canons be quit of toll and of all custom in all my burghs and throughout all my land, to wit, of all things that they buy and sell. And I forbid that any one take pledge on the land of the Holy Rood, unless the Abbot of that place shall have refused to do right and justice. I will moreover that they hold all that is above-written, as freely and quietly as I hold my own lands ; and I will that the Abbot hold his court as freely, fully, and honourably, as the Bishop of Saint Andrews, the Abbot of Dunfermline, and the Abbot of Kelso hold their courts. These being witnesses, Robert Bishop of Saint Andrews, John Bishop of Glasgow, Henry my son, William my nephew, Edward the Chancellor, Herebert the Chamberlain, Gillemichael the Earl, Gospatric the brother of Dolfin, Robert of Montague, Robert of Burnevile, Peter of Brus, Norman the Sheriff, Oggu, Leising, Gillise, William of Graham, Turstan of Crectun, Blein the Archdeacon, Aelfric the Chaplain, Waleran the Chaplain.

Nat. MSS Scot., i, No. xvi ; *L.C.*, No. cliii

THE STRUGGLE FOR ECCLESIASTICAL INDEPENDENCE

The Scottish church had its parishes and its dioceses, but it lacked that larger unit into which the church generally was now divided—the province, ruled by an archbishop or metropolitan, whose functions included the confirmation of the election of bishops in his province. In the absence of a Scottish metropolitan, authority over Scotland was claimed by the English archbishops, especially York. The following letter of Pope Calixtus II to the Scottish bishops in 1119 was one of many in which the pope commanded the Scottish bishops to submit to York.

1119.

Calixtus, bishop, servant of the servants of God, to all the bishops throughout Scotland, suffragans of the church of York, greeting and apostolic benediction. A certain grave and perilous presumption is said to prevail in your parts, to wit that, without consulting your metropolitan and other fellow-bishops, one is consecrated as bishop by another. . . . Therefore by apostolic authority we command you that none be consecrated henceforth as bishop in your churches except by your metropolitan the archbishop of York, or by his permission. Moreover we instruct and command your fraternity that setting every pretext aside you offer canonical obedience to our venerable brother Thurstan, consecrated archbishop of York by God's grace, and as if by the hands of St Peter ; even as in the time of Gerard, archbishop of the same church, was commanded by the lord of holy memory our predecessor, pope Paschal. And if you obey our commands may the divine mercy keep you and lead you to eternal life.

S.A., 137

When William the Lion accepted the king of England as his feudal superior by the treaty of Falaise (*infra*, p. 77), a renewed attempt was made to subject the Scottish church to the English. The following extract shows that the Scottish bishops declined to commit themselves, and suggests that they were able to take advantage of the rivalry of Canterbury and York.

1176.

And to the aforesaid council which was held at Northampton [in 1176] came William, king of Scotland, by mandate of the lord king ; and brought with him Richard bishop of St Andrews, and Joscelin bishop of Glasgow, and Richard bishop of Dunkeld, and Christian bishop of Galloway, and Andrew bishop of Caithness, and Simon de Thouni bishop of Moray, and the abbots and priors of his land to make subjection to the church of England.

Then the lord king demanded of them that by the faith which they owed him and by the oath which they had sworn to him they should make to the church of England the same subjection as they ought to make, and used to make in the time of the kings of England his predecessors. And they replied to him that their predecessors never made any subjection to the church of England, and that neither ought they to make any to her.

To this replied Roger, archbishop of York, that the bishops of Scotland had made subjection to the metropolitan church of York in the time of their predecessors ; and expressly the bishop of Glasgow and certain other bishops of Scotland ; and in support of this showed sealed documents which he had at hand concerning it.

Then a great dispute arose between Roger, archbishop of York, and Richard, archbishop of Canterbury, about the receiving of that subjection. For the archbishop of Canterbury said that the subjection ought to be made to the church of Canterbury, and the archbishop of York said, to his church. And thus ended that conference.

And the aforesaid bishops of Scotland received permission from the lord king and returned. And thereafter they sent their ambassadors secretly to Alexander, the chief pontiff, requesting that he would receive them in his own hand, and protect them from the subjection which the English church demanded of them.

Benedict of Peterborough, *Gesta Regis Henrici II*, i, 111 (*S.A.*, 264-5)

The church's long struggle for independence of York was won in 1192, when Pope Celestine III recognised the Scottish church as a ' special daughter ' of the Roman see, subject to no archbishop. The bull has been attributed to Clement III in 1188, but among the reasons for regarding 1192 as the correct date are : (1) This recognition of ecclesiastical independence was more likely to follow than to precede the treaty (or more correctly quit-claim) of Canterbury of 1189 (see *infra*, p. 79). That treaty itself made no provision for ecclesiastical independence although the treaty of Falaise (*infra*, p. 77) had provided for ecclesiastical subjection. (2) Confirmations by later popes refer to a bull of Celestine, but not to one of Clement. (See also *Chronicle of Holyrood*, Scot. Hist. Soc., 160-1).

The original bull of 1192 is known only from its appearance in English chronicles (*S.A.*, 299), but the re-issue by Honorius III in 1218, almost verbally identical with the first bull, is preserved in the Register House, and a translation of it is given here—

1218.

Honorius, bishop, servant of the servants of God, to his dearest son in Christ Alexander, illustrious king of Scots, and his successors forever. While all the faithful ought to find at the apostolic see patronage and favour, yet it is fitting that those should more especially be cherished by the defence of its protection whose faith and devotion have been tried in most things, that they may be so much the more incited to the fervour of love for it, and be subdued by the more devout affection of reverence for it, as they know that they have more surely attained a pledge of its benevolence and grace. For this reason, dearest son in Christ, considering the reverence and devotion towards the Roman church which we know you and your predecessors to have had from times long past, by the page of this present writing (following the example of Celestine and Innocent, our predecessors of happy memory, popes of Rome) we most strictly forbid that it be permitted to anyone except the pope of Rome or a legate sent from his side to publish a sentence of interdict or excommunication in the kingdom of Scotland, because the Scottish church (in which these episcopal sees are known to exist—St Andrews, Dunblane, Glasgow, Dunkeld, Brechin, Aberdeen, Moray, Ross and Caithness) is subject to the apostolic see as a special daughter, with no intermediary ; and if such a sentence be pronounced, we decree it invalid. We add, also, that it be not permitted to any henceforth who is not of the kingdom of Scotland to exercise the office of legate in it unless one whom the apostolic see has specially sent from its body for that purpose. We forbid, too, that disputes which may arise in the same kingdom about its possessions be carried to the judgment of arbiters placed outside the kingdom, unless on appeal to the Roman church. And if any writings come to light which have been obtained contrary to the decree of this liberty, or chance in future to be obtained, without mention made of this concession, let nothing result to the prejudice of you or your successors, or of your kingdom, concerning the grant of this privilege. Besides, the liberties and immunities granted by the Roman church to you and your kingdom and the churches in that kingdom, and hitherto observed, we have confirmed and decree that they remain unimpaired in time to come, saving the authority of the apostolic see. Let it be permitted to no man at all to infringe this writing of our grant, prohibition and confirmation, or venture rashly to transgress it. But if any presume to attempt this, let him know that he shall incur the wrath of Almighty God and of the blessed Apostles Peter and Paul. . . . Given at the Lateran by the hand of Ranerius, vice-chancellor of the holy Roman church, xi Kal. Decembris, the 7th indiction, the year of the Lord's incarnation MCCXVIII, and the third year of the pontificate of Honorius III.

Nat. MSS Scot., i, No. xlvii

Although the independence of the Scottish church from England was now recognised, it was not equipped with any organ of government as a province. The Fourth Lateran Council (1215) [1] laid down that metropolitans should hold provincial councils yearly to correct abuses, to reform morals, and to enforce the statutes of general councils. But Scotland had no metropolitan, and the Scottish clergy had hitherto met in provincial council only when summoned by a papal legate. Clearly, the question of providing machinery was now an urgent one. The following bull gave the necessary permission to hold a Scottish provincial council, and, although it was not in form perpetual, its provisions were followed down to 1472.

1225.

Honorius, bishop, servant of the servants of God, to his venerable brethren all the bishops of the kingdom of Scotland, greeting and apostolic benediction. Certain of you lately made known to our ears that since you had not an archbishop by whose authority you might be able

---

[1] One of the series of general councils of the western church, the fourth of them to be held at the Lateran church of St John in Rome.

to celebrate a provincial council, it happens in the kingdom of Scotland, because it is so remote from the Apostolic See, that the statutes of the General Council [1] are disregarded and very many irregularities are committed and remain unpunished. Now since provincial councils ought not to be omitted, in which care should be had, in the fear of God, to correct excesses and to reform morals, and in which the canonical rules should be read over and recorded—especially those which were laid down in the same general council—we command you, by apostolic writing, that, since you are known not to have a metropolitan, you celebrate a provincial council by our authority. Dated at Tivoli. 14 Kalends of June. In the ninth year of our pontificate.[2]

Robertson, *Statuta*, ii, No. 1

It remained to regulate the procedure of the Scottish general councils, and this was done in the following thirteenth-century statutes.

We, the prelates of the Scottish church, . . . ordain that every year all bishops and abbots and priors of priories shall religiously assemble . . . for the holding of a council on a certain day to be duly intimated to them by the conservator of the council ; so that they may be able to remain at the same council for three days, if need be. . . .

And we ordain firstly that every year the duty of preaching be laid on one of the bishops one after the other, [to be performed] at the next council by himself or by another to be proposed [by him], beginning with the bishop of Saint Andrews ; and that by choice of the others one of the bishops be appointed conservator of the statutes of the council.[3] . . .

Patrick, *Statutes of the Scottish Church*, 9

---

[1] The Fourth Lateran Council, of 1215   [2] 19 May 1225
[3] His title later became ' Conservator of the privileges of the Scottish Church.'

CHAPTER FIVE

FEUDALISM

With the accession of David I a feudal administration for the kingdom of Scotland was steadily introduced. Possibly such an administration had been initiated by Alexander I, but with the reign of David charters begin to multiply, providing us with evidence of feudal tenures, feudal law and feudal administration. In all this David relied largely upon the help of Anglo-Normans : they received grants of land from the king in feudal form and for a return of feudal services ; they formed the officers of the king's household ; and they became royal officials, like sheriffs and justiciars. At this time, too, we begin to hear of burghs, and we are told by one chronicler that they also were ' largely inhabited by English.'

With sheriffs holding the king's castles in the outlying parts, with a feudal nobility holding land of the king, bound by ties of loyalty to the crown, and giving to the king ' aid and counsel ' in the *curia regis,* and with the administration of a feudal law based upon the king's writs emanating from a central chancery, the component parts of the old Scotland were gradually welded together to form one kingdom of Scotland.

c. **1124.** *Charter by King David granting Annandale to Robert de Brus.*

[This is one of the earliest charters of David I. It is significant in its address—*Francis et Anglis* ; in its grant of Annandale *et suum castellum*—a grant which looks like the erection of a march fief ; in the reference to the *consuetudines* which Randolf Meschin had in Carlisle—presumably feudal *consuetudines* ; and in the names of the witnesses, who are mainly important English barons.]

David dei gratia rex Scottorum omnibus baronibus suis et hominibus et amicis Francis et Anglis salutem. Sciatis me dedisse et concessisse Roberto de Brus Estrahanent et totam

terram a divisa Dunegal de Stranit usque ad divisam
Randulfi Meschin ; et volo et concedo ut illam terram et
suum castellum[1] bene et honorifice cum omnibus consuetudinibus suis teneat et habeat, videlicet cum omnibus
illis consuetudinibus quas Randulfus Meschin unquam
habuit in Carduill et in terra sua de Cumberland illo die
in quo unquam meliores et liberiores habuit. Testibus
Eustachio filio Johannis et Hugone de Morvilla et Alano
de [Perci] et Willelmo de Sumervilla et Berengario Enganio
et Randulfo de Sules et Willelmo de Morvilla et Hervi
filio Warini et Edmundo camerario. Apud Sconam.

L.C., No. liv.

Abstract

David, King of Scots, grants to Robert de Brus Estrahanent
[Annandale] and all the land from the boundary of Dunegal of
Stranit [Nithsdale] to the boundary of Randolf Meschin. Brus
is to hold that land and its castle with all its customs, viz. all the
customs which Randolf Meschin ever had in Carlisle and in his
land of Cumberland on the day when he held them most fully.

1164 × 1174. *Charter by King William granting Annandale to
Robert de Brus.*

[This charter, granted to Robert de Brus, son of the preceding
Robert de Brus, illustrates the gradual process of definition in
feudal holdings. It also provides early references to the pleas of
the crown, to knight-service, and to castle-ward.]

Willelmus rex Scottorum episcopis abbatibus comitibus
baronibus justiciis vicecomitibus ceterisque probis hominibus
tocius terre sue Francis et Anglis Scottis et Galwahensibus
clericis et laicis salutem. Sciant presentes et futuri me
reddidisse et concessisse et hac carta mea confirmasse
Roberto de Brus et heredibus suis totam terram quam pater

---

[1] Lochmaben

suus et ipse tenuerunt in valle de Anand per easdem divisas per quas pater suus eam tenuit et ipse post patrem suum : Tenendam sibi et heredibus suis de me et heredibus meis in feudo et hereditate in bosco et plano in pratis et pascuis in moris et mareisis in aquis et stagnis et molendinis in forestis et tristiis in saltubus et portubus in viis et semitis in piscariis et omnibus aliis justis pertinenciis suis ita libere et quiete plenarie et honorifice sicut pater suus vel ipse eam tempore regis David avi mei vel regis Malcolmi fratris mei liberius et quietius plenius et honorificencius tenuit exceptis regalibus que ad regalitatem meam spectant scilicet causa de inventione thesauri causa de murdra causa de assaltu premeditato causa de femina efforciata causa de arsione causa de rapina quas causas mihi reservavi. Concedo etiam ei ut hee cause sint atacheate per unum hominum [*sic*] de feudo suo quem elegero et tractate et placitate per ante justicias meas infra comitatum de...[1] et tales consuetudines capiet de hominibus regni mei quales capiuntur apud Rokesburc excepta asisa baronie sue. Volo itaque . . .[1] predictus Robertus de Brus . . .[1] de me et heredibus meis . . .[1] libere sicut superius divisum est per servitium x militum excepta custodia castellorum meorum unde ipsum quietum clamavi. Testibus : Engelramo episcopo de Glasgu, Christiano episcopo de Withern, Ricardo de Morvilla constabulario, Waltero filio Alani dapifero, Odenello de Umframvilla, Henrico Luvel, Huctredo filio Fergusii, Gilberto filio Fergusii, Roberto filio Truite, Waltero de Windlesouer, Waltero Corbet, Gileberto filio Richardi, Rollando filio Huctredi, Willelmo de Haia, Willelmo de Mortemer, Rogero de Munethov, Simone Locard, Hugone clerico meo, Roberto de Chartres, Ricardo clerico. Apud Lochmaban.

Nat. MSS Scot., i, No. xxxix

[1] MS torn

Abstract

William, King of Scots, grants and confirms to Robert de Brus and his heirs all the land which his father and himself held in Annandale by the same boundaries by which his father held it, and he himself after his father. To be held by him and his heirs of the King and his heirs, in fee and heritage ; in wood and plain ; in meadows and pastures ; in moors and marshes ; in streams, ponds and mills ; in forests and trists [1] ; in woodlands and harbours ; in roads and paths ; in fishings ; and with all its just pertinents as freely as his father or himself held that land in the time of King David my grandfather and King Malcolm my brother, except the royal rights which pertain to my royal prerogative, viz. treasure trove, murder, premediated assault, rape, arson and robbery ; which pleas I have reserved to myself. I also grant to him that these pleas shall be attached [2] by one man of his fief whom I shall choose, and brought and pleaded by him before my justices within the earldom of . . . and he shall take such customs from the men of my realm as are taken at Roxburgh, except the assize of his barony. I wish the said Robert de Brus to hold of me and my heirs freely . . . as is laid down above by the service of ten knights, without ward of my castles from which I have quit-claimed him.

HOMAGE AND FEALTY

A prominent feature of feudalism was the relationship of lord and man, and in that relationship much depended upon good faith. So the tenant by military service entered into a solemn and sacred bond, with an impressive ceremony called homage, whereby he undertook to aid and support his lord against all others— though, if his lord were not the king, with the saving clause, ' except the faith that I owe to the king.'

The oath of fealty, taken at the time of homage or taken alone, was less solemn and less binding.

[1] Hunting-stations, or places where hounds are posted in a deer drive

[2] That is, the person accused shall be arrested, or ordered to compear before the court.

Memorandum that on St Baldred's day [6 March] in the year of grace 1269 [1270] Andrew son of Gilmour Clerauch of Dull did homage to lord John of Haddington prior of St Andrews within the priory of St Andrews on bended knees, placing his hands within the hands of the prior in the presence of Thomas vicar of Dull and William de Clatti and John de Norham younger canons, and there he swore, touching the Gospels, that he would hold faithful homage to the prior and convent and that he had never, and by right could never, do homage to any other than the prior and convent.

Register of St Andrews, 349

The manner in which a vassal ought to swear fealty

I, *A*, swear on these holy gospels of God that henceforth I shall be faithful to *B*, as a vassal ought to be to his lord, nor shall I, conscious that it is to his harm, reveal what he has entrusted to me under the name of fealty ; that I shall exalt him as much as I can ; that he shall never lose life or limb nor the honour which he has by my will, advice or encouragement, but in all these things I shall be his helper according to my power.

Register of Moray, No. 299

I, *A*, swear on these holy gospels of God that from this hour till the last day of my life I shall be faithful to you, *B*, my lord, against every man except the King. I swear that I shall never knowingly take part in council, battle, deed or conspiracy in which you shall lose your life or receive any hurt, injury or insult to your person or in which you shall lose any honour which you now have or shall have in the future ; and if I know or hear of anyone who wishes to do any of those things against you I shall do all that is in my power to render it harmless ; and if I am not able to cope with the danger I shall announce it to you when I can, and shall give you my help against it as I am able ; and if by wrong or by chance you shall lose anything which you have or shall have I shall help you to recover it, and having recovered it to retain it for all time ; and if I know that you justly wish to go against anyone and, for this, am requested specifically or generally, I shall provide you with my help as I can ; and if you show anything to me in secret I shall reveal it to no-one without your permission, nor have it revealed ; and if you ask advice of me on any deed I shall give you the advice which seems to me most expedient for you ; and I shall never knowingly do anything in my own person to bring harm or insult to you.

Register of Moray, No. 300

THE JURY

In the twelfth and thirteenth centuries the Scottish kings developed the use of the jury both for judicial work and for administrative purposes. The jury was used, for example, to decide the heir to lands and offices, to determine boundaries, to bring in verdicts (*veredicta*, or true sayings) in civil causes, and, as an assize (*assisa*) to determine criminal causes. The procedure was simple. The king's chancery directed a brieve (a writ, written *brevi manu*) to the local official (usually the sheriff) ordering him to inquire into the facts by upright and faithful men of the locality. Thereafter, in certain cases (retourable brieves) in which the king was interested in the decision (e.g. the heir to lands) the official sent in to chancery the finding (the return, or *retour*) of the jury, sealed with his seal and, later, with the seals of the jury. (See, in general, *Sheriff Court Book of Fife*, Intro., pp. lxxxvi–ci.)

Brieve of Alexander III directed to the sheriff of Forfar ordering him to determine, by a jury, the heir to Simon in the office of gatekeeper of the castle of Montrose.

21 March 1262.

A[lexander] by the grace of God king of Scots to Robert de Monte Alto [Mowat] his beloved and faithful sheriff and his bailies of Forfar, greeting. We command and order you that by upright and faithful men of the country [*patria*, i.e. the locality or legal 'country'] you diligently and faithfully cause inquiry to be made if Margaret, Agnes, Swannoch, Christina, and Marion, daughters of the late Simon, gate-keeper of Montrose, are the lawful and nearest heirs of the said late Simon in the land of Inyaney and in the office of gate-keeper of our castle of Montrose, and if the said late Simon died vest and seised as of fee in the said land and office. And when you have diligently and faithfully enquired into all these things, and also into the value and reasonable extent of the aforesaid land, you shall cause [the findings] to be sent to us as quickly as possible, together with this brieve.

A.P.S., i, 100 (from the original)

Retour of the Jury

This is the enquiry made, by order of the lord king, by Robert of Monte Alto [Mowat], knight, into the land of Inianey adjacent to Falerikkum—to wit, by these barons : the baronies of old Montrose, Rossyn, Fethyn, Kynel, Inverkilerd, Inverlunan, Kynbladmund, Lexyn, Dun, Brechyn, Kinabir Parva, Pert, Melgund, Pannemor, Panbride, Tunryn, and Roscolbyn, and a great part of the upright burgesses of Montrose. All of these aforenamed having taken the oath say that a certain man [who was] called Crane had and held the said land heritably by gift of king William and died vest and seised of the said land as of fee. And after his death, Swayn, his son, held and had the said land heritably and died vest and seised of the said land as of fee. And after his death, Simon, his son, held and had the said land heritably and died vest and seised of the said land as of fee. And that the said Simon had five daughters by two wives, to wit, Margaret, Agnes, Swannoch, Christina and Marion. And that the said Crane, Swayn and Simon never did military service or gave aid or did anything else in the world for the said land except [performing] the office of gate-keeper of the castle of the lord king at Montrose. And on oath they say that the said

women are the lawful and nearest heirs of the said Simon
who is now dead.

A.P.S., i, 100 (from the original)

Inquest on the death of William de Abercrumby's ancestor

An inquest made at Abercrumby on the Saturday preceding the Feast of the Apostles Simon and Jude [26 October],
1270, by the prior of Pittenweem, lord Richard Chamberlain, knight, William, lord of Anstruther and other free
and lawful men of the country [*patria*]. All these aforewritten say on oath that William son of the late Richard
of Abercrumby is lawful and nearest heir of the said
Richard of Abercrumby in the land of Abercrumby with
its pertinents, and say that he is of lawful age. They also
say that the said land of Abercrumby with its pertinents
in demesnes, returns, homages, services, dowers, fermes, and
in other things, is worth yearly, with the said pertinents,
34 merks of silver. They also say that Balcormok returns
the service of one tenant with a hauberk. They also say
that it does Scottish service for one and a half davachs of
land. Also half the land of Weston which pertains to the
said land of Abercrumby returns to the lord of that tenement yearly one pair of plain spurs or four pennies. They
also say that the land of Staynton returns yearly to the
lord of the fee one pound of pepper or twelve pennies ;
and they say this faithfully and truthfully on the oath
which they made. Moreover the said prior and Richard
Chamberlain put their seals to this inquest together with
the seal of the bailie.

A.P.S., i, 102 (from the original)

Inquest on the death of Adam the Miller

On the Monday immediately following the Feast of
St Fabian and St Sebastian [20 January] inquest was made
regarding Richard, son of Robert, the son of Elias, in the
castle of Dumfries in the presence of the bailies of the
lord king by the oaths of [here follow thirteen names] and

others. Who say that the aforesaid Richard and Adam the Miller met on the Sunday immediately following the Feast of St Michael [29 September] at the Church of the aforesaid saint and there, in the cemetery, the said Adam the Miller defamed the said Richard, giving him the name of thief, that is, ' Galuuet,' and the said A[dam] said that he would make the said [Richard] leave the town. Further it so happened that on the following Thursday the said R[ichard] passed down the street when the said A[dam] stood in the doorway of a certain house. Then a certain woman said to the same A[dam], ' Get back. Look, here is Richard.' The said A[dam] answered, ' I won't get back ; I have a knife as sharp as his.' Then the said A[dam] entered a certain house and took out a knife to stab the said R[ichard] in the bowels ; and the said R[ichard], to defend himself, drew his sword and struck A[dam] with the side of the blade. Then the said A[dam] put his arm round the sword and the said R[ichard] seized the sword and wounded the said A[dam] and thereby he died. Then the said R[ichard] declared, ' Look here ; I haven't killed you ; you killed yourself.'

The barons who were on oath agree on all points with the burgesses who were on oath. Also, the burgesses and other men of the barony say that in all things the said R[ichard] was a faithful man, but that Adam, on the other hand, was a thief by repute.

A.P.S., i, 97–8 (from the original)

The Sheriff

Although the earliest original Exchequer Roll now extant is dated 1326, we are fortunate in possessing a transcript, made for the first Earl of Haddington (1563–1637), which gives *inter alia* extracts from Exchequer Rolls of the years 1264 to 1266 and 1288 to 1290. The following extracts from the account of the sheriff of Ayr, rendered in 1266, have been taken from this Haddington transcript (printed in *Exchequer Rolls*, i, 1–51). They show the multifarious duties of the sheriff as a financial, administrative, judicial and military officer of the king.

From the account of William, earl of Meneteth, late sheriff of Ayr : Received—Item, by two parts of the earldom of Carrick which the earl of Buchan holds at ferm of that term, £56 6s 1d. Item, by the revenue of the sheriff, besides the bishop of Glasgow's eighth (which is 8s 4d), 58s 4d. [Expenses :] To a crossbowman of that year, 2 merks and a half. Item, in food and service of two watchmen of that term, 20s. Item, in food and service to the gatekeeper in that term, 8s. Item, in repair of buildings in the castle of Ayr, 27s. And in expenses of scouts spying on the king of Norway, three times, 24s 8½d. And in expenses of MacAngus MacDonald, a hostage, for twenty-six weeks, with a nurse and another maidservant, 79s 10d. And to four men watching the lord king's ships for 23 weeks, 16s 10½d. Item, in three dozen staves of yew, bought for the use of the crossbowman, 13s 4d. And in salt bought for the provisioning of the castle, 20s. Item, in ten chalders of oat meal for the said provisioning, £10. Item, in six chalders of corn bought for the said provisioning, £9 3s. And of £17 16s 5d for cows taken from the men of Kyle and Carrick (who detained as much from their ferm for the term of Martinmas foresaid). Item, for forty-six cows taken for the lord king's service at Brewevill, £9 4s. And so he owes £204 8s 3½d. Received of him—in corn from the provisioning of the castle of Ayr, 6 chalders.

Memorandum that the said earl has the son of Gilaverianus, who was farmer of the Cumbraes, as pledge for the composition which the said Gilaverianus made with the lord king, of 80 cows, until he shall pay the said cows.

The said earl craves that there be allowed to him the customs of 220 etc. stones of iron, the making of 1,770 quarrels and the making of 180 iron bolts. Item, he craves that there be allowed to him £60 15s 8d, which he expended in the construction of the lord king's ships at Ayr, and 7 merks which he expended in the cutting of 200 oars, the making and carriage thereof. And likewise he craves that there be allowed to him the expenses of 120 men whom he kept in the castle of Ayr for three weeks, in default of the burgesses, who ought to have entered the castle for its defence, according to the king's command, and the said earl says that they would not do so ; if this can be proved, the said burgesses are to pay to the said earl the expenses of the said men, otherwise the said earl is to pay the same expenses.

E.R., i, 5-6

LEGAL PROCEDURE

The Scottish kings in the twelfth and thirteenth centuries undoubtedly borrowed much from the administration and legal procedure of England. The following decision of the Kings' Council looks much like a borrowing of the procedure of indictment laid down in Henry II's *Assize of Clarendon*. It is also interesting for its statement that Galloway had ' special laws ' ; and we know that Galloway was still resisting the introduction of the jury in the reign of Robert I and that ' special laws ' were still claimed for it as late as 1384. The reference to the ' Justice of Lothian ' indicates that at this time the justiciar for Lothian included Galloway within his jurisdiction ; later there were separate justiciars for Lothian, Galloway and ' Scotland ' (that is, the country north of the Forth and Clyde). Murder and robbery are here referred to as ' pleas of the crown ' ; at this time the pleas of the crown were four in number—murder, robbery, rape and arson. It should be borne in mind, however, that this decision is found only in later legal collections, and that we do not possess the original record.

Of stablyssing of indytementis

The yer of grace mccxliiii apon the Mononday next eftir the fest of Sancte Scolastik the virgyn,[1] Alysandir, kyng of Scottis, stablyst and ordanit with the consal, adviz and consentment of the worshipfull faderis D. and W., of Sanct

[1] i.e. 13 February 1244-5

Androis and Glasgw bischopis,[1] Huchon, abbot of Kelcow, Robert, abbot of Dunfermlyn, Philip, abbot of Jedwart, Patrick, erle of Dunbar, R., erle of Wyntoun and constable of Scotland, W., erle of Albemerle, Waltir Comyn, erle of Menteth, M., erle of Strathern, Alisandir Comyn, erle of Buchane, William, erle of Mar, Johne the Balyole, Robert the Bruys, Henry the Balyole, chamerlayn, Roger of Moubray, Nichol of Soulis, William of Brechyn, Waltir of Petyn, Aymer of Maxwell and mony uthir erlis, baronis and worthi men of his kynryk, that his justice of Loutheane sal tentably and prively mak inquest for til inquyr of the mysdoaris of the land and of thair anerdaris [2] and resettouris be the athis of iii or iiii worthi and leill men and with the aith of the stewart of ilk toun of the schirefdome within his bailyery, outane in Galloway, the quhilk hes special lawys wythin thaim. And gif be that inquest lely made ony man be fundin endytit, hastily throu the kyngis serjandis with the help of the men of the toun thai sal be saufly attachit that at a certane daye and sted throu a lele assyse thai sal passe ; sa never the les that gif ony of thaim be convikyt be that assyse of murthir or of reyfflake [3] or of othir suylke felonyis that pertenis to the kyngis croune al thar catale but ony gaynsaying sal remayn to the kyng, and gif ony man be convikyt of theft or of manis slauchter or of ony suylke crime than al the gudis and catale of sic folk suld remayn with the lorde of the lande that thai wyn in wythout ony gaynsaying.

A.P.S., i, 403

The King's Council in action

One of the feudal burdens upon land was that of suit of court. Those who held land direct of the king owed suit to the sheriff's court of the sheriffdom in which their lands lay—likewise suit to the justice-ayre when it was held within the sheriffdom, and suit

---

[1] David de Bernham, bishop of St Andrews, and William de Bondington, bishop of Glasgow.

[2] *accomplices* [3] *robbery with violence*

to the king's own court, the *curia regis*. In a like way the tenant owed suit to his lord's court, there to give his lord aid and counsel. The suitors formed the ' body ' of the court ; they were the judgment-finders in legal causes ; and they drew up the rules and regulations (later known as the ' styles and statutes ' of the court) governing the general administration of the lord's lands whether the lord was lord of a barony or king of a kingdom. This entry also illustrates the use of the jury to ascertain certain facts, and the ' pyramid of appeal ' from sheriff to justiciar, and from justiciar to the King's Council.

Liability for Suit to the Sheriff Court of Perth

In the year of grace 1255 when David de Lochore then sheriff of Perth sought from the abbot and convent of Dunfermline four merks to the king's use for [their] default of suit to the sheriff court of Perth from their lands of Fordun, Cupermacultin, Bendhautine, Kethekerbege, Incheturfin and Dunmernech, at length, at the instance of the same abbot and convent, the lord king caused an inquest to be made by many baronies before Alexander Comyn, Earl of Buchan, then justiciar of Scotland, whether the said suit ought of right to be made from these lands or not. When the said inquiry had been diligently and faithfully made into this matter, Gilbert de Hay, knight, who had been one of the said inquest, pronounced in the full council [*colloquium*] of the lord king held at Holyrood on the twentieth day after Christmas in the same year [14 January 1256] that the verdict of the baronies was that they sometimes saw men from the aforesaid lands coming to the said court but that they never came there as suitors. On account of this, the lord king in the full council aforementioned by common consent of his magnates there present entirely quitclaimed the abbot, convent and their men in perpetuity from doing the aforesaid suit.

Register of Dunfermline, No. 58

The Burgh

David I may be said to be the founder of the Scottish burgh. The burgh was a strong-point, but it was also a centre for trade. Trade depends upon peace ; the burghs helped to secure peace for trade. The burgh was erected or created by the king, by a formal legal act ; but in origin it was often a new settlement of new men by the king's castle. It was a ' built-up ' area, and the burgess had to build his toft within a certain fixed period and had to reside there. The early burghs, as centres of trade, were usually given a monopoly of trade over a certain area (the ' trade-precinct ') which at first was the area of the sheriffdom. All trade within the sheriffdom had then to be conducted in the burgh. Only the king could create or authorise the creation of a burgh—as, for example, when David I granted leave to the canons of Holyrood to have a burgh between their church of Holyrood and the king's burgh of Edinburgh, or gave leave to the bishop of St Andrews to erect a burgh at St Andrews. Most of the early burgh charters refer to trading privileges, and to the right of holding a market and a fair, In these early charters, the use of the words *communio, communitas, communicare,* seems to indicate the idea of a community, which later became clarified as a corporation.

The Burgh of the Canongate

1128 × 1136. Concedo et eis herbergare quoddam burgum inter eandem ecclesiam et meum burgum et concedo ut burgenses eorum habeant communionem vendendi res suas venales et emendi in foro meo libere et absque calumpnia et consuetudine sicut mei proprii burgenses et prohibeo ne aliquis in burgo eorum panem vel cervisiam aut pannum aut aliquod venale capiat per vim aut sine voluntate burgensium.

L.C., No. cliii (cf. *supra*, p. 50)

Translation

And I grant to them [a right] to build for residential purposes a burgh between the same church [Holyrood] and my burgh

[Edinburgh] and I grant that their burgesses shall have rights enjoyed in common of selling their saleable goods and of buying in my market freely and without challenge and without [paying petty] custom, just like my own burgesses ; and I forbid anyone to sell in their burgh bread or ale or cloth or any other saleable commodity either by force or contrary to the will of the burgesses.

The Founding of the Burgh of St Andrews

1144 × 1153. Robertus Dei gratia Sancti Andreae humilis minister universis fidelibus tam futuris quam praesentibus salutem. Innotescat dilectioni vestrae nos Deo auxiliante et licentia regis nostri David burgum apud Sanctum Andream in Scotia statuisse et in ipso burgo hunc Mainardum Flandrensem cum regis consensu et ejus firma pace praefectum fecisse et huic praefato Mainardo et heredibus suis in ipso burgo propter suum servitium nobis et nostris fideliter exhibitum tres toftas scilicet a vico burgendi usque ad rivum prioris libere et quiete ab omni consuetudine pro sedecim nummis scilicet uniquique virgatae terrae quatuor denarios concedimus, quia ipse ex prioribus est qui burgum supradictum aedificare et in-staurare incepit. Eapropter successoribus nostris humiliter supplicamus quatenus illum et heredes suos pro amore Dei et Sancti Andreae et nostri diligant et manuteneant et nullus ei et suis super excommunicatione Dei et Sancti Andreae et nostri injuriam inferat et si quis ei quacunque ex causa injuriam fecerit rex terrae ei propter Deum rectum facere non diferrat quod si ipse non fecerit Rex Regum justus et aequus Judex in die magnae ultionis ei rectum faciat. Supradicta enim villa elemosina illius benedicti regis est et ipse supradictus Mainardus ejus proprius burgensis in Berrewyk fuit quem Sancto Andreae et nobis cum supradicta elemosina in elemosinam tribuit. His testibus Priore ecclesiae ejusdem villae Willelmo Torreld.

L.C., No. clxix

Abstract

Robert, bishop of St Andrews, makes it known that by leave of King David [I] he has erected a burgh at St Andrews ; that with the king's consent he has made Mainardus, the Fleming, the provost of the burgh ; and that he has given to Mainardus and his heirs, for faithful service, three tofts in the burgh to be held for sixteen *nummi*, namely four pennies for each virgate of land. And this he has done because Mainardus was one of the first to build and stock the burgh. Wherefore he commends Mainardus and his heirs to his successors in the bishopric, and to the protection of the king ; for it was the king who granted to him [the bishop] the *villa* of St Andrews to be held *in elemosina*, and who gave him Mainardus, who was the king's own burgess of Berwick, a gift likewise made *in elemosina*.

Charter of King William to Inverness

W[illelmus] dei gratia Rex Scottorum omnibus probis hominibus totius terre sue clericis et laicis salutem. Sciant presentes et futuri me omnes burgenses meos de Inuernis quietos clamasse omni tempore a tolneio et omni consuetudine per totam terram meam Quare prohibeo firmiter ne quis ab eis de eorum dominicis catallis tolneium aut aliquam consuetudinem exigat super meam plenariam forisfacturam Prohibeo etiam ne quis emat aut vendat in burgo illo aut in vicecomitatu illo extra burgum aliquam mercaturam exerceat nisi fuerit burgensis aut stalagarius eiusdem burgi aut per gratum burgensium hoc fecerit Dedi etiam et concessi predictis burgensibus ad sustentamentum burgi terram illam que est extra burgum que vocatur Burch halev scilicet que est inter montem et aquam Ita quod nullus in ea wannagium faciat aut pasturam habeat nisi per eorum licentiam Burgenses vero universi mihi conuentionauerunt quod cum circa predictum burgum fossatum fecero ipsi super fossatum totum burgum claudent bono palitio et ex quo clausum fuerit palitium illud sustentabunt et semper bonum et integrum conseruabunt. Teste M. Episcopo Aberdonensi. Comite Dunecano justiciario.

Ricardo de Moreuill constabulario.   Waltero Olifer.
Philippo de Valloniis.   Hugone Giffard.   Rogero de Valloniis.   Roberto de Berkelei.   Apud Eren.

A.P.S., i, 88 (from the original)

Translation

William, by the grace of God, King of Scots, to all upright men
of the whole of his land, both clergy and laymen, greeting.
Let all men, present and to come, know that I have freed all my
burgesses of Inverness for all time from the payment of toll and
all custom throughout the whole of my land.   Wherefore, under
pain of complete forfeiture, I firmly forbid any man to exact toll or
any kind of custom from them in respect of their own proper
goods.   I also forbid any man to buy or sell in that burgh, or in
that sheriffdom outwith the burgh, or to deal in any merchandise,
unless he is a burgess or a stallanger of that burgh or is one
permitted to do so by consent of the burgesses.   Also I have given
and granted to the aforesaid burgesses that land outwith the
burgh which is called Burch Halev—namely the land lying between
the hill and the water—to help them to maintain the burgh ; and
no one is to farm on that land or to have pasture there without
their permission.   Moreover the whole of the burgesses have
come to an agreement with me that when I have made an
[earthen] dyke around the aforesaid burgh they will enclose their
burgh with a sound palisade, erected on that dyke, and when
their burgh has been thus enclosed they will maintain the palisade
and keep it in good and sound repair.   Witness, etc.

CHAPTER SIX

RELATIONS WITH ENGLAND

If ' Scotland ' was to expand it could expand only southwards. A policy of southern expansion under Malcolm III received a stimulus through the Norman Conquest of England, which brought the legitimate claimant to the English throne, Edgar Atheling, and his sisters Margaret and Christina, to the Scottish court, and through the marriage of Malcolm and Margaret. The Atheling was certainly associated with two big risings in the north of England, and Malcolm himself invaded northern England in 1069–70. Doubtless with a view to establishing a firmer hold over the northern parts and also with a view to clarifying his relationship with the Scottish king, William the Conqueror invaded Scotland in 1072.

1072. The [Norman] French went into Scotland ; and took away with them as hostage the king of Scotland's son.[1]

Annals of Ulster, ii, 24 (E.S., ii, 34)

1072. In this year king William led a ship-force and a land-army to Scotland, and lay about that land with ships on the sea side ; and he himself with his land-army went in over the Forth. And he found there naught of which he was the better.

And king Malcolm came and made peace with king William, and gave hostages, and was his man ; and then [William] went home with all his army.

Anglo-Saxon Chronicle, MSS D, E (S.A., 95)

In 1079 Malcolm again invaded England and devastated Northumbria as far as the Tyne, which was now adopted as the English defensive line. William replied by sending his son Robert Curthose against the Scots.

[1] Duncan, son of Malcolm by his first wife, Ingibjorg

74

1080. In this year in the autumn-time . . . king William sent his son Robert to Scotland against Malcolm. But when he had come to Falkirk he returned without accomplishing anything, and founded a new castle upon the River Tyne.

Symeon of Durham, *Historia Regum*, ii, 211 (*S.A.*, 103)

Malcolm's fourth invasion of England, in 1091, again brought retaliation, and, with it, the establishment of an English strongpoint at Carlisle which, being in Cumbria, was probably regarded by Malcolm as part of the land which was his (see *supra* p. 14).

1092. In this year king William with a great army went north to Carlisle, and restored the town and built the castle ; and drove out Dolfin,[1] who ruled the land there before. And he garrisoned the castle with his vassals ; and thereafter came south hither, and sent thither a great multitude of [churlish] folk [2] with women and cattle, there to dwell and to till the land.

Anglo-Saxon Chronicle, MS E (*S.A.*, 108)

The seizure of Carlisle was undoubtedly one of the factors leading to Malcolm's final invasion of England in 1093, and his death at Alnwick. The expansionist policy was for a time abandoned. The sons of Malcolm and Margaret—Edgar, Alexander I and David—maintained amicable relations with King Henry I (1100–35). They owed their position on the throne partly to English intervention, which had helped them to overthrow Donald Bane, first in the interests of Duncan II and then in the interests of Edgar ; and Henry I married their sister. Yet Edgar's decision that Alexander's kingdom should consist of Scotland north of the Forth, while David, as earl, held the southern lands over which England might claim superiority, suggests Scottish apprehension about English claims—probably to Lothian ; and Ranulf Flambard's foundation of a castle at Norham, in 1121, shows that although the Scots no longer held land to the south

---

[1] Son of Gospatric, Earl of Dunbar
[2] *Cyrlisces.* In *Annals of Waverley* the reading is *multos villanos.*

of the Tweed the English had no confidence that they had relinquished their claims to it.

Once again the stimulus to Scottish aggression came from internal dissensions in England. On Henry's death in 1135, Stephen attempted to establish himself as king, to the prejudice of Matilda, daughter of Henry and niece of King David. The Scots invaded England in 1136 and 1138 and, although defeated at the battle of the Standard, continued operations which were ended by the treaty of Durham (1139), confirming Northumberland (except the castles of Bamborough and Newcastle) to Scotland. Matilda left England in 1148, and in the next year David came to an understanding with her son, Henry.

1149. And Henry,[1] son of Matilda the empress, now a youth of sixteen years, nourished in the court of David, king of Scots, the [uncle] of his mother,[2] was knighted by the same king David in the city of Carlisle; he having first given an oath that, if he became king of England, he would give to [David] Newcastle and all Northumbria, and would permit him and his heirs to possess in peace without counter-claim for ever the whole land which lies from the river Tweed to the river Tyne.

Hoveden, *Chronica*, i, 211 (*S.A.*, 221)

David died in 1153. He had been predeceased by his son, Henry, and was succeeded by his grandson, Malcolm IV. Thus when Matilda's son became king of England as Henry II on Stephen's death in 1154, he had to deal not with David (to whom he had made his promise in 1149), but with a boy of thirteen. Henry II was one of the ablest kings England ever had, and in 1157 Malcolm was induced or compelled to give up all claim to the northern parts of England in return for a confirmation of his rights in Huntingdon.

[1] Later, 1154, Henry II, King of England
[2] Matilda, sister of David I and daughter of Malcolm III, had married Henry I, and their daughter Matilda had married firstly, Henry V, the Emperor, and secondly, Geoffrey of Anjou, the son of the second marriage being Henry [II of England].

To the king of Scots also, who possessed as his proper right the northern districts of England, namely Northumbria, Cumberland, Westmoreland, formerly acquired by David, king of Scots, in the name of Matilda, called the empress, and her heir, [king Henry II] took care to announce that the king of England ought not to be defrauded of so great a part of his kingdom, nor could he patiently be deprived of it : it was just that that should be restored which had been acquired in his name.

And [Malcolm] prudently considering that in this matter the king of England was superior to the merits of the case by the authority of might, although he could have adduced the oath which [Henry] was said to have given to David, his grandfather, when [Henry] received from him the belt of knighthood ; when [Henry] asked them again, restored to him the aforenamed territories in their entirety, and received from him in return the earldom of Huntingdon, which belonged to him by ancient right.

William of Newburgh, *Historia Rerum Anglicarum* (*S.A.*, 239)

William ' the Lion ', of different mettle from Malcolm IV, ' hoping to make old losses good by a new conflict,' [1] joined in the conspiracy against Henry II headed by the latter's son, Prince Henry, who promised William Northumbria as far as the Tyne.[2] William invaded England in 1173 and 1174, but at Alnwick was surprised by the English under cover of a mist. Taken prisoner, he was sent to Falaise, in Normandy, where he made the following treaty with Henry II.

William, king of Scotland, has become the liege man of the lord king against every man, for Scotland and for all his other lands ; and has done him fealty as to his liege lord, as his other vassals are accustomed to do to him. Similarly he has done homage to king Henry, his son ; and fealty, saving his faith to the lord king, his father.

And all bishops and abbots, and the clergy of the land

[1] *E.S.*, ii, 277   [2] *S.A.*, 246

of the king of Scotland, and their successors, shall do to the lord king, as to their liege lord, fealty for all for which he wishes to have it, as his other bishops are accustomed to do to him ; and to king Henry, his son, and to their heirs.

And the king of Scotland, and David, his brother, and the barons and his other vassals, have conceded to the lord king that the church of Scotland shall make to the church of England henceforth such subjection as she ought to make to her, and used to make in the time of the kings of England, his predecessors.

Similarly Richard, bishop of St Andrews, and Richard, bishop of Dunkeld, and Geoffrey, abbot of Dunfermline, and Herbert, prior of Coldingham, have conceded also that the church of England shall have that right in the church of Scotland which by right she ought to have ; and that they will not oppose the right of the church of England. . . .

And in token to the lord king, and to Henry, his son, and to his heirs, of the sure observance by the king of Scotland and his heirs of this agreement and compact, the king of Scotland has delivered to the lord king the castle of Roxburgh, and the castle of Berwick, and the castle of Jedburgh, and the castle of Maidens,[1] and the castle of Stirling, at the mercy of the lord king. . . .

Moreover in token of the fulfilment of the aforesaid agreement and compact, the king of Scotland has delivered up to the lord king his brother David as hostage, and earl Duncan, and earl Waldeve [*and several others*].

And when the castles have been rendered, William, king of Scotland, and David his brother shall be released. . . .

Moreover the bishops, earls and barons have pledged themselves to the lord king and to Henry, his son, that if by any chance the king of Scotland should draw back from fealty to the lord king and to his son, and from the aforesaid agreement, they shall hold with the lord king, as with their liege lord, against the king of Scotland, and

[1] i.e. Edinburgh Castle

78

against all men who oppose the lord king. And the bishops shall place the land of the king of Scotland under an interdict, until he return to fealty to the lord king.

Lawrie, *Annals*, No. xlv ; *S.A.*, 260–3

The masterful Henry II died in 1189, and his successor was Richard Coeur-de-Lion. Richard's primary objective was participation in the third crusade, and to help to finance his expedition he sold back to Scotland, for 10,000 merks of silver, the rights acquired by his father by the treaty of Falaise. This agreement restored the position as it was before 1174, but left open the undefined English claim to overlordship which had existed previously. It is in the form of a feudal charter of quitclaim whereby a superior renounces certain rights or services previously due from his vassal.

Richard, by God's grace king of England, duke of Normandy and Aquitaine, count of Anjou, to the archbishops, bishops, abbots, earls and barons, justiciars, sheriffs and all his bailiffs and vassals, greeting.

Know that we have restored to our dearest cousin William, by the same grace king of Scotland, his castles of Roxburgh and Berwick [1] as his own, to be possessed by him by hereditary right and by his heirs for ever.

Moreover we have freed him from all compacts which our good father Henry, king of England, extorted from him by new charters, and by his capture : so to wit that he do to us fully and entirely all that Malcolm, king of Scots, his brother, did to our predecessors of right, and of right ought to have done ; and that we do to him all that our predecessors did of right to Malcolm aforesaid, and ought to have done ; namely, in the matter of conduct when he comes to court and while he stays at court, and when he returns from court, and in his provisionings [2] and in all his liberties, dignities and honours rightfully due. . . .

[1] Edinburgh had been restored to William by Henry ' when by his wish and counsel he took a wife from foreign parts ' (*S.A.*, 307, *note* 1).
[2] cf. *infra*, p. 95

Moreover concerning the lands which he may have in England, whether in demesne or in fee, to wit in the county of Huntingdon and in all others, let him and his heirs in perpetuity possess them in the same liberty and fullness as the aforesaid king Malcolm possessed or ought to have possessed them ; unless the aforesaid king Malcolm or his heirs shall have afterwards enfeoffed anything ; yet so that whatever has since been enfeoffed, the services of those fiefs shall pertain to him and to his heirs. . . .

We have restored also to him the allegiance which our father had received of his vassals, and all the charters which our father had of him through his capture. And if perchance any should be retained by oversight or be found, we command that they be wholly without validity.

And the oft-named king William has become our liegeman for all the lands for which his predecessors were liegemen of our predecessors ; and he has sworn fealty to us and to our heirs.

Foedera, i, 64–5 (Record edn., i, 50) ; Lawrie, *Annals*, 282–4 ; *Nat. MSS Scot.*, i, No. xlvi ; *S.A.*, 308–9

In the year 1190 [actually December 1189], William, the king of the Scots, gave to Richard, the king of the English, ten thousand marks of gold and silver for his dignities, and liberties, and honours, which he had had before the war ; and for Berwick and Roxburgh, which king Henry had forcibly retained during sixteen years. And so, by God's assistance, he worthily and honourably removed [Henry's] heavy yoke of domination and of servitude from the kingdom of the Scots.

Chronicle of Melrose (*E.S.*, ii, 322)

During most of the reigns of John and Henry III (1199–1272), England was hampered by internal dissension and was not aggressive towards Scotland. Alexander II married a sister, and Alexander III a daughter, of Henry III, and Anglo-Scottish relations were in the main amicable. There were still debateable marches between the two countries, as the first of the following documents illustrates, and the question of homage, though mainly in abeyance, remained unsettled. When claims to overlordship were seriously advanced by Henry III in 1236, Alexander II retorted with a counter-claim to the northern English counties. By the treaty of York, in the following year, Alexander abandoned his claim to the northern counties, receiving in return land in Northumberland and Cumberland worth £200 a year. The third document illustrates the achievement of a peace which was to last for over half a century.

1222. *A Perambulation of the Border*

Hugh de Bolebec to the King. Informs him that on the quinzaine of Michaelmas, being the day fixed by the King of Scotland, he with the knights of Northumberland met in person at Revedeneburne,[1] David de Lindesay, Justiciar of Lothian, Patrick Earl of Dunbar, and many other knights sent by the King of Scotland. The business on which they had met being opened, they elected six knights for England and six for Scotland, as jurors to make a true perambulation between the kingdoms, viz. between Carham and Hawedene.[2] Whereon the six English knights with one assent proceeded by the right and ancient marches between the kingdoms, the Scottish knights totally dissenting and contradicting them. Wherefore it was agreed between the justiciar and earl and the writer, to elect other twelve knights, six on either side, and associate them in the perambulation with the first twelve, for greater security. These being elected and sworn, the English knights agreed on their said boundaries, and the Scottish knights to different ones, as before. And inasmuch as the Scottish knights thus stood in the way of the business, the writer, in virtue of the King's command, elected and caused to be sworn twenty-four discreet and loyal knights of his county that they might settle the ancient marches between the kingdoms. These accordingly, on oath, declared the true and ancient marches between the kingdoms as follows, viz.

[1] Reddenburn, a tributary of the Tweed
[2] Howdean, near Jedburgh

from Tweed by the rivulet of Revedeneburne, ascending towards the south as far as ' Tres Karras '[1] and from thence in a straight line ascending as far as Hoperichelawe,[2] and from thence in a straight line to Witelawe.[3] But on their wishing to go thus, and beginning to make the perambulation, the foresaid justiciar and earl with their knights, resisting with violence, hindered them by threats from so doing. Whereupon the English knights, thus hindered, firmly asserted that the above were the true and ancient marches.

Bain's Calendar, i, No. 832

1237. Treaty of York

It was agreed

That the said Alexander king of Scotland remitted and quit-claimed for himself and his heirs to the said Henry king of England and his heirs in perpetuity the said counties of Northumberland, Cumberland and Westmoreland [*and fifteen thousand marks of silver which King John, father of Henry, received from William, former king of Scotland, father of Alexander, for certain agreements entered upon between the said kings which were not observed by King John, as Alexander king of Scotland says*] and all agreements made between King John and King William about marriages between Henry king of England or Richard his brother and Margaret or Isabella sisters of the said Alexander king of Scotland. . . .

For this remission and quitclaim the said Henry king of England gave and granted to the said Alexander king of Scotland two hundred librates of land within the said counties of Northumberland and Cumberland if the said two hundred librates of land can be found in these counties outside towns where castles are situated, and if any is lacking, it shall be made up in suitable places nearest the said counties of Northumberland and Cumberland ; to be had, held and retained in demesne by the said Alexander

---

[1] Unidentified   [2] Hoperiglaw   [3] Whitelaw

king of Scotland and his heirs the kings of Scotland of the said Henry king of England and his heirs ; rendering from it annually one red falcon to the king of England and his heirs at Carlisle through the hands of the constable of the castle of Carlisle whoever he may be on the feast of the Assumption of the Blessed Mary for all services, customs and other demands which might be exacted for the same lands. . . .

And the said king of Scotland shall do his homage from these lands to the said Henry king of England and shall swear fealty to him.

Foedera, **i**, 233

Results of peace on the Border, *1237*

Letter Close of Henry III.

As a firm peace has been entered upon between the King and the King of Scotland, so that the King is not now in fear of his castles as before, it is not necessary that there should be as great expense at the royal castles at Bamborough and Newcastle-on-Tyne as there used to be ; and Hugh de Bolebec is commanded to spend as little as he can on the maintenance of the aforesaid castles. . . .

Cal. Close Rolls, 1234–7, 498

CHAPTER SEVEN

SOCIAL AND ECONOMIC CONDITIONS

We know very little of social and economic conditions in Scotland prior to the reign of David I. A tantalising glimpse of the organisation of Celtic society is provided in the *notitiæ* written in the margins and blank pages of the *Book of Deer*; but it is a glimpse and nothing more. Thus the evidence to be derived from occasional passages in such works as Adamnan's *Life of St Columba* (written before 704, and probably completed in 691) and Turgot's *Life of Queen Margaret* (written before 1115) is all the more valuable. Three such passages are given below.

With the reign of David I, however, and the evidence of feudal charters and writs, some further, but still very slight information becomes available.

Extracts from Adamnan's ' Life of St. Columba,' illustrating conditions in the days of the Columban monks

Twice three bushels of barley . . . being sent to the peasant, Findchan by name, according to the Saint's [Columba's] command, and set down before him, . . . he thankfully accepted them, saying : ' How can a crop mature if sown after midsummer, contrary to the nature of this land ? ' His wife, on the other hand, says : ' Do according to the Saint's command. . . .' The messengers also at the same time added this, saying, ' Saint Columba, who sent us to thee with this gift, gave also by us this command about thy crop, saying : " Let that man trust in the omnipotence of God ; his crop, although sown fifteen days before the beginning of the month of June, shall be reaped in the beginning of the month of August." ' The peasant obeys, ploughing and sowing ; and the crop, which he sowed against hope at the time above mentioned, he gathered in, ripe, in the beginning of the month of August, . . . to the wonder of all his neighbours.

Book ii, ch. iii

At another time, when the Saint was staying for some days in Ireland, . . . he mounted a car, previously blessed by him and yoked, but, through some unaccountable oversight, without the necessary linch-pins being first inserted in the holes at the axle-ends. . . . There was on that day a great strain on it over long stretches of road, without the wheels and the axles falling asunder or becoming loose, although, as has been said above, there were no linch-pins to hold them together or steady them.

Book ii, ch. xliii

After this the Saint goes out of the granary, and, returning towards the monastery, sits down half-way at the place where afterwards a cross, fixed in a millstone, and standing to this day, is to be seen at the roadside. And . . . behold the white horse, a faithful servant, runs up to him, the one which used to carry the milk pails to and fro between the byre and the monastery. He, coming up to the Saint, wonderful to relate, lays his head against his breast . . . knowing that his master would soon leave him, and that he would see him no more, began to whinny and, like a human being, to shed copious tears into the lap of the Saint.

Book iii, ch. xxiii

Extract from Turgot's ' Life of Queen Margaret,' showing how her influence upon Scotland stimulated foreign trade

Also this noblest jewel of royal race made the magnificence of royal honour much more magnificent for the king ; and she conferred very great glory and honour upon all the nobles of the kingdom and their attendants. For she had caused merchants to come by land and sea from various regions, and to bring very many precious wares that were still unknown there. As an instance of this the natives compelled by the queen bought clothing of different colours, and various ornaments of dress. Arrayed at her instigation in different refinements of dress, they bore themselves so that they seemed to have been in some sense

85

reformed by this elegance. . . . She multiplied also the adornments of the royal palace, so that not only was it resplendent with various adornment of silken cloths, but even the whole house glittered with gold and silver. The vessels in which food and drink were brought to the king and the nobles of the realm were either made of gold or silver or overlaid with gold or silver.

ch. 7, translated in E.S., ii, 68

NATIVI OR SERFS

It is difficult to assess the social status of the *nativus* or serf in Scotland in the twelfth and thirteenth centuries. The first of the following three documents shows that the fugitive serf could be brought back to the land and the lord whence he had fled ; the second and third documents show that a serf and his family could be either lent or given away like a chattel. On the other hand it is noticeable in the second document that the agreement is made between the serf himself and the convent of St Andrews (not between James, son of Morgound, and the convent) ; and that the serf and his family must have been possessed of worldly goods if they were to provide a pound of wax annually.

There seem to have been differing grades of serfs attached to the land, some being of a much lower status than others. Probably those of higher status had some admitted rights in the land to which they were attached ; but on that the records are silent.

Mandate by King David I for the return of fugitive serfs to the Abbey of Dunfermline, c. 1126

David, king of Scots, to all his faithful men of the whole of Scotland and Lothian, greeting. I command that *cumerlache* [1] be speedily restored to the church of the Holy Trinity of Dunfermline, and all the serfs whom my father, mother and brothers gave to it, and its *cumerlache* from the time of King Edgar until now, with all their money,

---

[1] Evidently a term meaning fugitive serfs

wherever they be found ; and I forbid that they be unjustly detained.

L.C., No. lxx

Agreement for the loan of a serf, 1222

This agreement was made between the lord S., prior of St Andrews, and convent thereof, on one side, and Gillemor Scolgo of Tarualont, their liege man and serf, on the other, namely that the said Gillemor, as their serf and liege man, shall, with their licence, be with lord I., son of M.,[1] of good memory, late earl of Mar, as long as it please the said prior and convent, on condition that the said G. and his children with all their substance shall, when it please the said prior and convent, return to them as their serfs, without contradiction or hindrance from anyone, and the prior and convent shall in good faith assign them a suitable place in which to dwell. If G. or his children remain with the said lord I. for a year or more, they shall pay to the prior and convent yearly, in recognition of their homage, 1 lb. of wax on the Assumption of St Mary. And because the said G. had not a seal of his own, he caused this agreement to be sealed with the seal of the said lord I., son of M., earl of Mar. For greater security, the said G., touching sacred things, swore faithfully to observe this agreement in good faith and without any contradiction.

Antiq. Aberdeen and Banff, ii, 18–19

Grant of a serf and his family, 1258

To all who shall see or hear this writ, Malise, earl of Strathearn, everlasting greeting in the Lord. Know ye all that I, moved by charity, for the salvation of my soul and of those of my ancestors and successors, have given, granted and by this my charter quit-claimed of me and my heirs for ever to God and to St John, Apostle and Evangelist, and to the abbot and convent of Inchaffray, in pure and

---

[1] James, son of Morgound (*Scots Peerage*, v, 569)

perpetual alms, John, called Starnes, son of Thomas, son of Thora, with all his children ; and for me and my heirs for ever I grant to the said abbot and convent all right and claim which I have or which I or my heirs may have in future in the said John or his offspring, and I forbid all my men to dare to cause interference, injury or any other hindrance to the said John or any of his offspring. In witness whereof . . .

Charters of Inchaffray, No. lxxxviii

SHEEP FARMING, COAL AND SALT

The Cistercian Order, which believed in a balance of prayer and work, and which was introduced into Scotland by David I, did much to improve Scottish agriculture ; and Cistercian houses are usually to be found on good farming land.

The monks of Melrose, in the Tweed valley, were great farmers and sheep-breeders, and the following extracts from their charters illustrate not only the extent of their flocks [1] and the arrangements for the pasturing and herding of the sheep, but also their overseas trade in wool with the Low Countries.

The charters granted to the monks of Newbattle (another Cistercian house) show that they were working coal, quarrying, and distilling salt. Salt distilled in saltpans, however, proved to be unsuitable for preserving meat and fish, and great quantities of salt were imported, mainly from Hamburg and the Baltic ports.

Excerpt from an agreement between the monks of Melrose and Earl Patrick of Dunbar, 1208

The earl . . . granted to them [the monks] pasture, to be possessed for ever, for five hundred sheep and seven

---

[1] Earl Patrick of Dunbar granted rights to the monks of Melrose to pasture three flocks of sheep, each flock numbering five hundred (*Liber de Melros*, No. 56) ; Elena de Moreville and her son Roland of Galloway gave them pasturage for seven hundred ewes with their followers of two years, or as many wedders (ibid., No. 82) ; in Wedale the monks had pasturage for five hundred sheep (ibid., No. 101) ; and in Priamside pasturage for four hundred sheep (ibid., No. 146).

score cattle, namely oxen and cows, as it shall please them, within the wood and without, everywhere between the way leading towards Loweder by the causeways (which way is called Malcholmisrode) and Leder and from the bounds of Cadesley to Fauhopeburne ; reserving to the earl and his heirs the trees in the wood only. It is agreed also between them that neither the monks nor the earl or his heirs shall have houses or sheepfolds or fences or shelters or folds or other erections within the said pasture, nor shall it be ploughed by any of them except the arable land called Sorulesfeld, which belongs to the monks by the said earl's gift ; nor shall the earl's beasts cross the said way, nor shall he or his heirs or his men claim any right beyond it ; and the earl's beasts shall each night return to the town of Hercheldune unless hindered by storm or flood ; and it is to be understood that the monks' beasts (from the nearest cowsheds and folds) shall have free entry and exit to and from their pasture.

Register of Melrose, No. 101

Charter by Richard de Moreville to the monks of Melrose

To all sons of holy mother Church, Richard de Moravilla, constable of the king of Scotland, and William, his son and heir, greeting. Know ye that we have granted and by this our present charter confirmed to God and the church of St Mary of Melrose and the monks serving God there, for the souls of us and of all our ancestors and successors, the place in Witelej within the margin of the forest, to make a cowshed for 100 (that is, six score) cows, or a sheepfold, whichever shall seem better and more useful to them . . . and a house in which they may make a fire for the brethren and their herds, and also a house in which they may place their hay. These three houses to be made in the foresaid place of Witelei we have granted in pure and perpetual alms to the said monks to be enjoyed for ever.

Ibid., No. 106

The Protection of Philip, Count of Flanders

I, Philip, count of Flanders and Belgium, wish it to be known to those present and those to come that, for the safety of my soul and the souls of my ancestors, I have granted to the brothers of Melrose and of their houses every kind of liberty of travelling safely through all my land. Wherefore I command and firmly order all my men and servants to whom these letters shall come that, as they love me and my honour, they dare not to exact from the aforesaid brothers any toll or any custom at all on land or in harbour. Moreover, if perchance dissension shall arise for any reason between the merchants of England and Flanders, no one shall seize the opportunity to dare to lay hands on the foresaid brothers, or to take away any of their property as a pledge. Anyone, therefore, who does injury or harm to the aforesaid brothers in my land, let him know that he incurs my wrath and that I will be avenged.

Register of Melrose, i, No. 14

Grant of a coal-working to the abbey of Newbattle, early thirteenth century

Seyr de Quency, earl of Winton, to all sons of holy mother church, greeting. Know ye that I have given and by this my charter confirmed to God and the church of St Mary of Neubotle and the monks serving God there, in pure and perpetual alms, for the increase of the alms which my father Robert granted to them in the territory of Travernent, namely all the half of the march extending from the west eastward to the burn of Wygtrig, to wit that part which is nearest to their cultivation ; moreover, the coal-working and quarry between the said burn of Wigtrig and the bounds of Pontekyn [i.e. Pinkie] and Invereske, and in the ebb and flow of the sea. And I will and command that none of my men within the bounds of the grange of Preston have any common, either in pasture, coal-working or quarry, without the goodwill of the said monks.

Register of Newbattle, No. 66

Grant of a saltpan at Callendar (Falkirk) by King Malcolm IV to the monks of Newbattle

Malcolm, king of Scots, etc. Let all present and to come know that I have granted, and by this my charter confirmed, to God and the church of Neubotle and the monks serving God there a saltpan in Kalentyr, gifted by King David,[1] my grandfather, and common easement in pastures and waters, and fuel for the said saltpan in the wood of Kalentyr, with common pasture, in perpetual alms, free and quit of all custom and secular service. Besides, I grant to them the whole arable land which they have in Kalentyr, free and quit in perpetual alms. Rendering therefor yearly to my bondsmen four shillings, two at Whitsunday and two at Martinmas.

Register of Newbattle, No. 163

Forest

By the king's charter (and later, apparently, by the feudal lord's own charter) lands could be erected into ' forest,' that is, into a preserve for game. Within the forest no-one could hunt, hawk, cut wood, build, graze cattle or till the land without leave of the holder of the forest. The forest, moreover, enjoyed forest law, which was stricter than the law of the land and which was enforced in forest courts—though Scotland never knew the detailed forest administration and the harsh forest law of the English royal forest. Thus it was vital to know what were the ' bounds ' of the forest and, for those holding land nearby, it was vital to ensure that their cattle did not accidentally stray into the forest.

c. 1185. *Roger Avenel with the consent of his overlord King William ' the Lion ' grants to Melrose all his land of Eskdale but he makes it known that*
I have only retained for myself and my heirs, deer and hind, boar and goat within the aforewritten bounds without

---

[1] David granted the saltpan *c.* 1142 (*L.C.*, No. cxlix).

damage or hurt to the crops, meadows, hedges, flocks, animals and all other possessions of the monks. But although I and my heirs shall have no forester within these aforesaid bounds, nevertheless we shall have within these bounds rights over thieves, and the nests of hawks and sparrow hawks and keepers to keep them and rights over trespassers. Be it known also that the foresaid monks shall have and possess all the foresaid land free and quit from me and my heirs, except my aforesaid game and nests of hawks and sparrow hawks. And they shall use all this tenement to their will and pleasure as best and most expediently seems to benefit them, their brothers, their servants and their flocks except that they shall not hunt there with packs of hounds and nets, nor lead others to hunt, nor place snares there except for catching wolves nor shall they take nests of hawks or sparrowhawks within these lands.

Register of Melrose, i, No. 39

MISCELLANEOUS

Charters are the only contemporary record we have for the legal, constitutional and social history of Scotland prior to the reign of Alexander III, and only fragmentary laws have been preserved prior to 1466 when the official register of Parliament begins. Much of the early law was local and customary, and there are occasional charter references to *assisæ terræ* which probably formed a common law. The following charter illustrates a custom and common law, protecting the rights of travellers.

Pasture for travellers, 1264

Alexander, by the grace of God king of Scots, to all good men of his whole land, greeting. Know ye that seeing how in the times of our ancestors the illustrious kings of Scots, and in our own time until now, it has been the usage throughout our kingdom of Scotland (according to ancient approved custom and by the common law) that both religious men and other persons, passing through the country with their vehicles, in whatever fief they arrived, might lawfully remain for one night in it, feeding their beasts there, saving standing corn and hay meadows, according to what we have learned plainly enough by the instruments and writings of our said ancestors ; we, willing that the said custom and common law be firmly observed, strictly forbid that any one, against this custom and common law, do harm, damage or injury to the monks of Melrose or other religious men, through whatever parts they happen to pass, or offer impediment to their free passage with their beasts and vehicles, pasturing without injury to standing corn and hay-meadows, on penalty of our full forfeiture. Witnesses : Hugh of Abirnithin, William Comin of Kelle-bride, John of Lambirton.   At Melrose the 21 day of July the sixteenth year of our reign.

Nat. MSS Scot., i, No. lx

Grant of eight oars in the ferry boat of Queensferry, 1276

Under the feudal system, offices, as well as lands, were granted by charter and were held ' in feodo et hereditate ' (that is, as a heritable fief), or for life, or for a term of years.   The following interesting letters patent show that an oar in the ferry boat at Queensferry could be the subject of a feudal grant and that sasine of the oar was to be given by the bailie.   Doubtless the right to an oar in the ferry boat was profitable.

A ferry across the Forth, provided by Queen Margaret, is referred to in Turgot's *Life,* and probably gave rise to the names of North Queensferry and South Queensferry.   Free ferrying ' at the Queen's ship ' was one of the privileges of the canons of St Andrews in 1183 (*Reg. of St Andrews,* 57), and the names *Portus reginæ* and *Passagium reginæ* are used in the second half of the twelfth century.   The right of the ferry was granted to Dunferm-line by Malcolm IV (*Reg. of Dunfermline,* No. 250) though both earlier and later documents refer to the right of Dunfermline as being only ' dimidium passagii Sanctæ Margaretæ Reginæ.'

To all who shall see or hear this writ, Ralph, by the grace of God abbot of Dunfermline, and humble convent thereof, everlasting greeting in the Lord. Know ye that we have given and granted to John *Armiger*, Peter, son of Adam, Thomas, son of Bernard, Richard of Kirkeland, Magota of Craggy, John Flokker and Eva, daughter of John Harloth, and their heirs, eight oars in the ferry boat called the new boat, in such a way that the said John *Armiger* and his heirs or assignees (except they be religious) have two oars of the said boat and each of the others have one oar. Besides, we grant to Susanna, spouse of the said John, that if she survive she have the said two oars for her lifetime and answer to us of their ferm yearly, and after her decease the said two oars are to revert to the heirs or assignees of the said John. To be held and had by her and the heirs or assignees of the said John *Armiger* (the two oars pertaining to him) of us and our successors peacefully and quietly ; rendering to us yearly 8d for each of the said eight oars, 4d at Martinmas and 4d at Whitsunday, and paying to our *firmarius* of Moehal for the time being what they were used to pay, and to the *firmarius* of the ferry the old ferm. And when any of them happen to die, the successor shall double the ferm, and doing us fealty shall have sasine of his oar by us or by our bailies. In witness whereof to this writ we have appended the seal of our chapter. Given at Dunfermline on the morrow of the Epiphany [7 January] in the year of grace 1275[/6]. Witnessed by the chapter.

Reg. of Dunfermline, No. 320

1266. *Provisions in the Treaty of Perth, between Scotland and Norway, 1266, concerning maritime losses*

If it happen (which God forbid !) that the men of the king of Norway suffer shipwreck in the kingdom or domain of the king of Scotland, or contrariwise, it shall be lawful for them, either in person or by agents, freely and quietly to gather their ships, broken or shattered, along with all their goods, and to have them, to sell and to dispose of them, without any claim, as long as they have not abandoned them. And if any one acts contrary to this act of common agreement concerning these goods or ships, fraudulently or violently abstracting from them, and is convicted thereof, let him be punished as a plunderer and breaker of the peace as he deserves.

A.P.S., i, 421 (from the ' Black Book ')

The allowance of money and provisions made to the Scottish kings on their attendances at the English court

Richard I, in 1194, *confirmed to William ' the Lion ' the rights which his predecessors had been accustomed to enjoy, in the following terms :*

For each day after he has, at our command, crossed the borders of his kingdom on his way to our court, 100 shillings sterling, and as much each day on his return journey from our court until he arrive in his own land. And for every day from his arrival at our court until his departure for his own land, 30s. sterling ; and 12 of our demesne wastels [1] and as many of our demesne simnels ; 12 sesters [2] of wine, viz. 4 of our demesne wine, with which we are served, and 8 of the wine from which our household is served ; two stones of wax, or four cakes of wax ; 40 of the demesne candles with which we are served, and 80 candles of those with which our household is served ; 2 lbs. of pepper and 4 of cumin. [3]

And he shall have, moreover, the escorts which his ancestors used to have coming to our court and returning from it, namely the bishop of Durham and the sheriff and barons of Northumberland shall meet him on the bounds

---

[1] Cakes or loaves made of the finest flour   [2] Casks
[3] An aromatic and carminative spice from the seeds of the plant *cummin cyminum.*

of his kingdom, shall receive him there and escort him as far as the Tees, and there the archbishop of York and the sheriff and barons of York shall come to him and shall receive him and escort him as far as the bishopric of Lincoln, and there the bishop of Lincoln and the sheriff and barons shall take him and receive him and [he shall be escorted] [1] through the jurisdictions by the sheriffs of the provinces through which he shall pass until he come to our court. . . .

Lawrie, *Annals*, 294 ; Bain's *Calendar*, i, No. 226

[1] MS is illegible at this point

SECTION II
1286–1424

Chapter Eight

DESCRIPTIONS OF SCOTLAND

Brevis Descriptio Regni Scotie

1292 × 1296.

In primis Tyndale continet xxx leucas [1] in longitudine et xx leucas in latitudine. Postea vero est Loudian de eisdem longitudine et latitudine. In Tindale sunt castra subscripta, Rokesborw, Geddeworthe. In Louthian sunt castra, Berewick, Edeneborw, Donbar, et Striuelyn. Iste due provincie extendunt se usque Erlesferie et Queneferie, id est, aqua xii leucas in latitudine et in alio loco ij leucas.

Postea est terra de Fif in qua est burgus Sancti Andree et castrum de Locres.[2] Est enim in longitudine xxx leucarum et in latitudine trium. Et tunc est i aqua longitudine ij leuce.

Et tunc est terra de Anegos latitudinis xx leucarum et longitudinis plus quam xxx. Et sunt ibi ij castra, Dunde et Forfare.

Et itaque est quoddam vastum quod vocatur, Le Mounth, ubi est pessimum passagium sine cibo, longitudinis lx leucarum et latitudinis xvj leucarum.

Postea est [terra] de Mar latitudine xxx leucarum et longitudine trium. Et plus deinde est terra de Bouwan [3] latitudine xxiiij leucarum et longitudine xxx leucarum. Et ibi . . . est burgus de Aberdene cum castro.

Deinde est terra de Morref latitudine xxiiij leucarum et longitudine xxx leucarum. Et ibi castrum de Elgyn et castrum de Spiny.

Et postea est terra de Ros latitudine xxiiij leucarum et longitudine xl et plus.

[1] Leagues   [2] Leuchars   [3] Buchan

Deinde est terra de Cateneys longitudinem xxiiij leucarum et latitudinem xl.

Deinde est terra de Orkenneye latitudine xiiij leucas et
longitudine xl leucas.

Item Novum castrum super Are in Orewin[1] prope
Galewey. In Galewey est Anandresdale terra domini
Roberti de Brus. Et postea est castrum de Dounfres regis
Scocie, Kirkudbrythe, Willelmi de Ferres, castrum de
Baleswyntoun,[2] Johannis Comin. Et est Galewey in
longitudinem lxx leucas et in latitudinem ubi plus est xxiiij
leucas.

Summa leucarum in longitudine v^c in latitudine cum
passagio aquarum ccc et xviij leucas.

Skene, *Chronicles of the Picts and Scots*, 214–15

Towns and Castles in Scotland in 1296

1296.

The following account of Edward I's progress through Scotland
as far north as Elgin, and then back again (by a partially different
route) shows that only once was the English king compelled to
sleep under canvas.

In the twenty-fourth year of the reign of King Edward of
England, Easter Day was on the day of the Annunciation
of our Lady [25 March] and on the Wednesday after
Easter, being the 28 day of March, King Edward passed,
in the forenoon, the river of Tweed, with 5000 horses
covered and 30,000 footmen, and lay that night in Scotland
at the priory of Coldstream ; and the Thursday at Hutton ;
and the Friday took the town of Berwick-upon-Tweed, by
force of arms, without tarrying. The castle was given up
the same day by Lord William Douglas, who was in it ;
and the king lay in the said castle all that night, and his
host in the town, every man in the house that he had
gained ; and the king tarried there almost a month.

[1] Irvine   [2] Dalswinton

And on St George's Day, the 23rd day of April, came news to the king that they of Scotland had besieged the castle of Dunbar, which belonged to the Earl Patrick, who holds strongly with the king of England. And on the Monday [23 April] the king sent his men to raise the siege, but before they came the castle was given up the same day. The Scots were in it when the English king's forces came to it, and besieged it with three hosts on the Tuesday [24 April] that they came there ; and on the Wednesday [25 April] they that were within sent out privily ; and the Thursday and Friday [26, 27 April] came the host of the Scots near them, just after noon, to have raised the siege of the Englishmen ; and when the Englishmen saw the Scots come toward them, then the Englishmen ran to the Scots and discomfited them ; and the chase lasted more than five leagues of way, until the hour of vespers. There died there Lord Patrick of Graham, a great lord, and 10,055 by right reckoning. The same Friday came the king from Berwick to go to Dunbar, and lay that night at Coldingham ; the Saturday [28 April] at Dunbar, and the same day those of the castle surrendered to the king's pleasure ; and there were in it the earl of Atholl, the earl of Ross, the earl of Menteith, Sir John Comyn of Badenoch, the son of Sir Richard Siward, Sir William of St Clair and as many as four score men of arms and seven score footmen. There the king tarried three days.

On Wednesday, Ascension Eve [2 May], the king went to Haddington, the Sunday after [6 May] to Lauder, the Monday [7 May] to Roxburgh, to the Greyfriars ; on Tuesday [8 May] he went to the castle [of Roxburgh] and remained there fourteen days. The fifteenth day, Wednesday [23 May] he went to Jedburgh, the Thursday [24 May] to Wyell, Friday [25 May] to Castleton, Sunday [27 May] back again to Wyell, Monday [28 May] to Jedburgh, the Friday after [1 June] to Roxburgh, the Monday after [4 June] to Lauder, Tuesday to Newbattle, Wednesday [6 June] to Edinburgh, to the abbey, and caused there to be set three engines casting into the castle day and night, until on the fifth day [11 June] they spoke of peace. On the eighth day the king went to his bed at Linlithgow, leaving the engines still casting in good order before the castle. The Thursday [14 June] he went to Stirling, and those who were in the castle ran away and left none but the porter, who rendered the castle ; and thither came the earl of Strathearn to the peace, and the king tarried there five days.

The Wednesday before St John's Day [20 June] the king passed the Scottish sea [1] and lay at Lutreard (*or* Outrear) [2] castle ; the Thursday [21 June] to St John's of Perth, a fine town, and there abode Friday, Saturday and Sunday, even St John the Baptist's day [24 June]. On Monday [25 June] the king went to Kinclevin castle, on Tuesday [26 June] to Clunie castle, and there abode five days. The Monday after [2 July] to Entrecoit [3] castle, Tuesday to Forfar, a castle and a fine town, the Friday after [6 July] to Farnell castle, Saturday [7 July] to Montrose, a castle and a fine town, and there remained Sunday, Monday and Tuesday. And there came there King John of Scotland to his mercy, and rendered wholly to him the kingdom of Scotland as one that had forfeited it. Likewise there came to mercy the earl of Mar, the earl of Buchan, Sir John Comyn of Badenoch and many others.

On Wednesday [11 July] the king went to Kincardine manor in Mearns, Thursday [12 July] into the hills at Glenbervie and Friday [13 July] to Dunes [Durris] manor among the hills. On Saturday [14 July] he reached Aberdeen, a fair castle and a good town upon the sea, and tarried there five days. And thither was brought his enemy, Sir Thomas Warham, whom Sir Hugh St John did take, and twelve with him. Friday after [20 July] he went to Kintore manor, Saturday [21 July] to Fyvie castle, Sunday [22 July] to Banff castle, Monday to Cullen manor, Tuesday in tents in Lannoy [4] on the river Spey. Wednes-

---

[1] The Firth of Forth   [2] Auchterarder
[3] Probably Inverqueich   [4] Probably Enzie

day [25 July] he passed, and came to the other side of the same river, to Rapenache manor, in the country of Moray ; on Thursday [26 July] to the city of Elgin, a good castle and fine town, and tarried there two days ; the Sunday [29 July] to Rothes manor. The same day the king sent Sir John de Cantelou, Sir Hugh Spencer and Sir John Hastings to search the country of Badenoch, and he sent the bishop of Durham with his people back over the mountains by another way than he went himself. The Monday [30 July] he went himself into Interkerach,[1] where there are no more than three houses in a valley between two mountains ; the Tuesday [31 July] to Kildrummy, a castle of the earl of Mar, and there remained over Wednesday, St Peter's day, and the beginning of August. On Thursday [2 August] to the hospital of Kincardine in Mearns ; Saturday [4 August] to the city of Brechin, Sunday [5 August] to the abbey of Arbroath—and it was said that the abbot made Scotsmen believe that there were only women in England ; Monday [6 August] to Dundee, Tuesday [7 August] to the red castle of Balledgarno, Wednesday [8 August] to St John of Perth, Thursday to the abbey of Lindores, where he remained over Friday [10 August], St Laurence's day. Saturday to the city of St Andrews, a castle and a good town, Sunday [12 August] to Markinch, where is but the church and three houses ; Monday to the abbey of Dunfermline, where nearly all of the kings of Scots lie ; Tuesday to Stirling, and tarried there on Wednesday, the feast of our Lady ; Thursday [16 August] to Linlithgow ; Friday to Edinburgh, and remained there Saturday ; Sunday to Haddington ; Monday [20 August] to Pinkerton near Dunbar ; Tuesday at Coldingham ; Wednesday at Berwick [22 August]. And he conquered the kingdom of Scotland and searched it through, as is aforesaid, in twenty-one weeks and no more.

Translated from the French in *Bannatyne Miscellany*, i, 271–81

---

[1] Innerquharanche

The Lowlands and Highlands of Scotland in the Fourteenth Century

c. 1380.

Scotia, also, has tracts of land bordering on the sea, pretty level and rich, with green meadows, and fertile and productive fields of corn and barley, and well adapted for growing beans, pease and all other produce ; destitute, however, of wine and oil, though by no means so of honey and wax. But in the upland districts, and along the highlands, the fields are less productive, except only in oats and barley. The country is, there, very hideous, interspersed with moors and marshy fields, muddy and dirty ; it is, however, full of pasturage grass for cattle, and comely with verdure in the glens, along the water-courses. This region abounds in wool-bearing sheep, and in horses ; and its soil is grassy, feeds cattle and wild beasts, is rich in milk and wool, and manifold in its wealth of fish, in sea, river and lake. . . . It also produces a good deal of iron and lead, and nearly all metals.[1]

Fordun, *Chronica Gentis Scotorum* (trans. Skene) II, viii

[1] Froissart, who was in Scotland in the reign of David II, wrote, ' There is neither iron to shoe horses, nor leather to make harness, saddles, or bridles : all these things come ready made from Flanders by sea ; and, should these fail, there is none to be had in the country ' (Hume Brown, *Early Travellers in Scotland*, 11). The evidence of the Exchequer Rolls shows that Scotland was a heavy importer of iron ; on the other hand, there was a considerable amount of primitive iron-smelting *in the Highlands* (*Proceedings of the Society of Antiquaries of Scotland*, xxi, 1886–7).

Chapter Nine

SCOTTISH INDEPENDENCE :
THE CROWN : FOREIGN RELATIONS

Treaty of Salisbury, 6 November 1289

On the death of Alexander III in 1286, his grand-daughter Margaret, ' The Maid of Norway ' (daughter of Eric II of Norway and Margaret, daughter of Alexander III), who had been acknowledged as Alexander's heir in 1284 (*supra*, pp. 33–4), became Queen of Scots. In 1289, while she was still in Norway (and then about six years old), her father, Eric, sent commissioners to Edward I of England to discuss the affairs of the infant Queen and her kingdom ; and, at the request of Edward I, the Scots sent commissioners to meet Eric's commissioners together with commissioners appointed by the English king, ' saving always the liberty and honour of Scotland.' The commissioners of the three countries met at Salisbury where the following treaty was concluded.

. . . That the aforesaid Queen and heir [of the kingdom of Scotland] shall come to the kingdom of England or Scotland, before the Feast of All Saints next to come [1 November 1290], free and quit of all contract of marriage and espousal ; and this the aforesaid Norwegian envoys promise faithfully they will cause to be done within the foresaid term, so far as in them lies, unless the Queen shall have therein some reasonable and permissible essoin.[1] . . .

The said king of England faithfully promises that if the aforesaid Lady shall come into his hands or custody free and quit of all contract of marriage and espousal, then, when the kingdom of Scotland shall have been fully settled in quietness and peace, so that the Lady herself may come there

[1] *excuse*

safely, and stay there, and when the king of England shall be so requested by the people of Scotland, the said king will send the same Lady to Scotland, as free and quit of all contracts, as is said above, as he received her.

Provided that the good people of Scotland, before they receive the Lady, shall give sufficient and good surety to the aforenamed king of England that they will in no wise marry the aforesaid Lady save with his ordinance, will and counsel, and with the assent of the king of Norway, her father.

And the aforesaid Scottish envoys likewise faithfully promised, for themselves and for others of the kingdom of Scotland, that they would establish quietness in the land of Scotland before the said Lady comes there ; and they would give surety that she should be able to come there with safety, as to her own kingdom, and freely to stay there of her own will, as true Lady, Queen and heir of that land. . . .

Foedera, i, 719–20

It will be noted that in the Treaty of Salisbury there was much stress upon the Maid of Norway being ' free and quit of all contract of marriage.' Unknown to the Scots, Edward I had already applied to Pope Nicholas IV for a dispensation for the marriage of Margaret and his son Edward [later Edward II] who were within the forbidden degrees of the canon law—

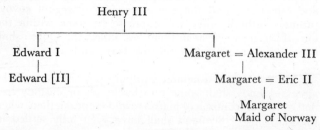

Henry III

Edward I   Margaret = Alexander III

Edward [II]   Margaret = Eric II

                                  Margaret
                                Maid of Norway

And, ten days after the Treaty of Salisbury was concluded, a dispensation for the marriage of Edward (son of Edward I) and

Margaret passed the papal seals (16 November 1289 : Rymer, *Foedera*, i, 721).

Nevertheless the Scots took no objection to Edward I's action. In a letter of 17 March 1290, sent from Birgham, the four surviving guardians (the Bishops of St Andrews and Glasgow, John Comyn and James the High Steward), ten other bishops of Scotland, twelve earls, twenty-three abbots, eleven priors and forty-eight barons speak of the joyous news of the granting of the dispensation and cordially agree to the marriage (*A.P.S.*, i, 441) ; and a letter was sent by the Scots to Eric II urging him to send his daughter to England (Rymer, *Foedera*, i, 731).

In July 1290 a new treaty was concluded between Scotland and England—a marriage treaty, but one which safeguarded the ' rights, laws, liberties and customs of Scotland ' ; though the saving clauses, inserted by England, are so ambiguous that it is difficult to understand how the Scottish plenipotentiaries came to accept them.

TREATY OF BIRGHAM 18 July 1290

(Confirmed at Northampton, 28 August 1290)

The more important clauses are :

We, having due consideration to the peace and tranquillity of both kingdoms, and that mutual affection should continue between their peoples for all time, have granted in the name and on behalf of our lord king [Edward I] and his heirs that the rights, laws, liberties and customs of the kingdom of Scotland in all things and in all ways shall be wholly and inviolably preserved for all time throughout the whole of that kingdom and its marches. Saving always the right of our lord king, and of any other whomsoever, which has pertained to him, or to any other, on the marches, or elsewhere, over these things in question before the time of the present agreement, or which in any just way ought to pertain to him in the future.

We expressly will and grant in the name of our lord king and his heirs, and in our name, that, failing heirs to the aforesaid Edward and Margaret, or either of them, in the event that the aforesaid kingdom [of Scotland] ought of right to return to the nearest heirs, it shall return and be restored to them, wholly, freely, absolutely and without any subjection,—if perchance in any way that kingdom shall happen to come into the hands of our lord king or his heirs,— and in such a way that, by reason of these presents, nothing shall accrue to our lord king, or his heirs, or any other, and, in a like way, nothing shall be lost. . . .

We promise in the name and on behalf of our lord king and his heirs that the kingdom of Scotland shall remain separate and divided from the kingdom of England, by its right boundaries and marches, as have hitherto in the past been observed, and that it shall be free in itself and without subjection ; saving always the right of our lord king, and of any other whomsoever, which has pertained to him, or to any other, on the marches or elsewhere . . . before the time of the present agreement, or which in any just way ought to pertain to him in the future. . . .

We expressly grant, for our lord king and his heirs, that the chapters of cathedral, collegiate, and conventual churches which hold their own elections shall not be compelled to pass outwith the kingdom of Scotland to seek leave to elect, or to present the persons elected, or to swear fealty or oath to the king of Scotland. And that no one holding in chief of the aforesaid king of Scotland shall be compelled to pass outwith the kingdom to do homage or fealty, or to pay the relief for his lands. . . .

No one of the kingdom of Scotland shall be held to answer outwith that kingdom for any agreement entered into, or for any crime committed, in that kingdom, or in any other cause, contrary to the laws and customs of that kingdom ; as has hitherto been reasonably observed. . . .

No parliament shall be held outwith the kingdom and marches of Scotland on matters touching that kingdom or its marches or the position of those who inhabit that kingdom. Neither shall any tallages, aids, hostings, or maletots be exacted from the aforesaid kingdom, or placed upon the people of the same kingdom, except to meet the expenses of the common affairs of the kingdom and in those cases where the kings of Scotland were wont to demand the same.

The Treaty ends with a final protestation :

We protest that all the clauses in this treaty are to be so understood that by this treaty the rights of neither kingdom are in any wise to be increased or decreased ; nor are the rights of either of the kings, but each king is to have his own estate freely.

Stevenson, *Documents Illustrative of the History of Scotland*, i, No. cviii.

LETTER OF BISHOP WILLIAM FRASER

1290. The Maid of Norway, however, died in September 1290, in or near the Orkney Islands, when on her way to Scotland ; and on 7 October 1290 William Fraser, bishop of St Andrews, wrote to Edward I announcing the rumoured death of the Maid, suggesting that Edward make a demonstration on the Borders to ensure the tranquillity of Scotland, and hinting that John Balliol, if set up as king, would follow Edward's counsel and would act to Edward's honour and advantage.

To the most excellent Prince and most revered Lord, Lord Edward, by the grace of God most illustrious King of England, Lord of Ireland, and Duke of Aquitaine, his devoted chaplain, William, by divine permission humble minister of the church of Saint Andrew in Scotland, wisheth health and fortunes prosperous to his wishes with increase of glory and honour. As it was ordered lately in your presence, your ambassadors and the ambassadors of Scotland who had been sent to you and also some nobles of the kingdom of Scotland met at Perth on the Sunday next after the feast of Saint Michael the Archangel to hear your answer upon those things which were asked and treated by the ambassadors of Scotland in your presence.

Which answer of yours being heard and understood the faithful nobles and a certain part of the community of Scotland returned infinite thanks to your Highness. And your foresaid ambassadors and we set ourselves to hasten our steps towards the parts of Orkney to confer with the ambassadors of Norway for receiving our Lady the Queen, and for this we had prepared our journey. But there sounded through the people a sorrowful rumour that our said Lady should be dead, on which account the kingdom of Scotland is disturbed and the community distracted. And the said rumour being heard and published, Sir Robert de Brus who before did not intend to come to the foresaid meeting, came with a great following to confer with some who were there. But what he intends to do or how to act, as yet we know not. But the Earls of Mar and Atholl are already collecting their army ; and some other nobles of the land are won over to their party and on that account there is fear of a general war and a great slaughter of men, unless the Highest, by means of your industry and good service, apply a speedy remedy. My Lords the Bishop of Durham, Earl Warenne and I heard afterwards that our foresaid Lady recovered of her sickness, but she is still weak ; and therefore we have agreed amongst ourselves to remain about Perth, until we have certain news by the knights who are sent to Orkney, what is the condition of our Lady, —would that it may be prosperous and happy ; and if we shall have the accounts which we wish concerning her and which we await from day to day, we will be ready to set forth for those parts, as is ordained, for carrying out the business committed to us to the best of our power. If Sir John of Balliol comes to your presence we advise you to take care so to treat with him, that in any event your honour and advantage be preserved. If it turn out that our foresaid Lady has departed this life (may it not be so), let your excellency deign if you please to approach towards the March, for the consolation of the Scottish people and for saving the shedding of blood, so that the faithful men of the kingdom may keep their oath inviolate and set over them for King, him who of right ought to have the succession, if so be that he will follow your counsel. May your excellency have long life and health, prosperity and happiness. Given at Leuchars on Saturday the morrow of Saint Faith the Virgin, in the year of our Lord 1290.

Nat. MSS Scot., i, No. lxx

CLAIMANTS FOR THE CROWN

Eventually thirteen competitors put forward claims to the Scottish crown. Their names and their pedigrees are given below. Edward I offered himself as arbitrator, provided the competitors acknowledged him as feudal superior of Scotland. That acknowledgment was made by nine of the thirteen competitors who, furthermore, agreed that sasine of the land and castles of Scotland should be given to Edward so that, when he made his award, he could give sasine of the land and castles to the rightful king.

The thirteen claimants were soon reduced to three—John Balliol, Robert Brus and John Hastings, the three descendants of the three daughters of David, earl of Huntingdon. Finally the Crown was awarded to John Balliol, as the descendant of the eldest daughter, though Robert Brus, descended from the second daughter, was one degree nearer to David I.

The Thirteen Competitors in 1291

Florent V, count of Holland, great-grandson of Ada, eldest daughter of Earl Henry, son of David I.

Patrick de Dunbar, 8th earl of Dunbar and 1st earl of March, great-grandson of Ada, illegitimate daughter of William 'the Lion'.

William de Vesci, grandson of Margaret, illegitimate daughter of William 'the Lion'.

William de Ros, great-grandson of Isabella, illegitimate daughter of William 'the Lion'.

Robert de Pinkeny, great-grandson of Marjorie, daughter of Earl Henry, son of David I.

Nicolas de Soules, grandson of Marjorie, illegitimate daughter of Alexander II.

THE THIRTEEN CLAIMANTS FOR THE CROWN

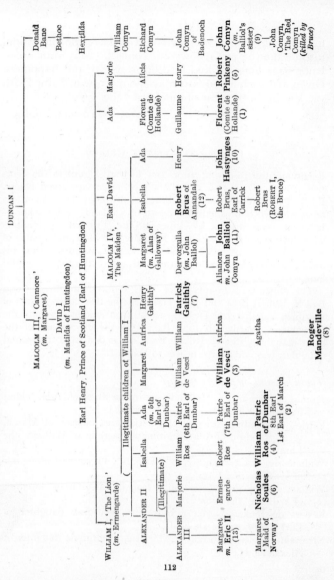

112

Patrick Galithly, son of Henry Galithly, an illegitimate son of William ' the Lion '.

Roger de Mandeville, great-great-grandson of Aufrica, illegitimate daughter of William ' the Lion '.

John Comyn, lord of Badenoch, great-great-grandson of Hextilda or Histilla, granddaughter of Donald Bane, king of Scots. [John Comyn married Alianora, sister of John Balliol, and his son was the Comyn murdered by Bruce in 1306.]

John de Hastynges, grandson of Ada, third daughter of David, earl of Huntingdon (younger brother of William ' the Lion ').

John de Balliol, grandson of Margaret, eldest daughter of David, earl of Huntingdon.

Robert de Brus, lord of Annandale, son of Isabella, second daughter of David, earl of Huntingdon.

Eric II, king of Norway, husband of Margaret, daughter of Alexander III and father of the Maid of Norway.

SUBMISSION OF THE COMPETITORS TO EDWARD I, ACCEPTING HIM AS SOVEREIGN LORD OF SCOTLAND, 5 AND 6 JUNE 1291

Edward, by the grace of God King of England, Lord of Ireland, and Duke of Aquitaine, to his beloved in Christ the Prior and Convent of Christ Church, Canterbury : greeting. We send to you, under the seal of our Exchequer appended to these presents, transcripts of certain letters which lie in our Treasury, containing the tenor which follows :—

To all who shall see or hear these letters, Florence Count of Holland, Robert de Brus Lord of Annandale, John Balliol Lord of Galloway, John de Hastings Lord of Abergavenny, John Comyn Lord of Badenoughe, Patrik de Dumbar Earl of the March, John de Vescy for his father, Nicholas de Soules and William de Ros, greeting in God. Seeing that we profess to have right to the kingdom of Scotland, and to set forth maintain and declare such right before that person who has most power, jurisdiction and reason to try our right ; and the noble Prince, Sir Edward by the grace of God King of England, has shown to us, by good and sufficient reasons, that to him belongs, and that he ought to have, the sovereign lordship of the said kingdom of Scotland, and the cognizance of hearing, trying and determining our right ; We, of our own will, without any manner of force or constraint, will, concede and grant to receive justice before him as sovereign lord of the land ; and we are willing, moreover, and promise to have and hold firm and stable his act, and that he shall have the realm, to whom right shall give it before him. In witness of this thing we have put our seals to this writing. Made and given at Norham, the Tuesday next after the Ascension, the year of grace one thousand two hundred and ninety-first.

To all those who shall see or hear this present letter, Florence Count of Holland, Robert de Brus Lord of Annandale, John Balliol Lord of Galloway, John de Hastings Lord of Abergavenny, John Comyn Lord of Badenoughe, Patrik de Dumbar Earl of the March, John de Vesci for his father, Nicholas de Soules and William de Ros, greeting in God. Seeing that we have conceded and granted of our good will and common consent, without any constraint, to the noble Prince, Sir Edward by the grace of God King of England, that he, as sovereign lord of the land of Scotland, may hear, try and determine our claims and our demands, which we purpose to set forth and declare for our right to the kingdom of Scotland, and to receive justice before him as sovereign lord of the land ; promising, moreover, that we shall hold firm and stable his act, and that he shall have the realm, to whom right shall give it before him : but seeing that the aforesaid King of England cannot take nor effect such manner of cognizance without judgment, and that judgment ought not to pass without execution, and that execution he cannot duly do without possession and sasine of the same land and of its castles : We will, concede, and grant that he, as sovereign lord, in order to effect the things aforesaid, have sasine of the whole land and of the castles of Scotland until right be done and performed to the claimants, in such manner that, before he have the sasine aforesaid, he give good and sufficient security to the claimants and to the guardians and to the community of the kingdom of Scotland, to make restitution of the same kingdom and of the castles, with all the royalty, dignity, lordship, franchises, customs, rights, laws, usages, and possessions, and all manner of appurtenances, in the same state in which they were when sasine to him was given and delivered, to that person who shall, by judgment, have the right to the kingdom, reserving to the King of England the homage of him who shall be king, so that the restitution be made within two months after the day when the right shall be tried and declared. And that the issues of the same land in the meantime received be safely deposited and well kept in the hands of the Chamberlain of Scotland who now is, and of him who shall be associated with him on the part of the King of England, and under their seals, saving the reasonable maintenance of the land and of the castles and of the officers of the kingdom. In witness of these things foresaid, we have put our seals to this writ. Made and given at Norham, the Wednesday after the Ascension, the year of grace one thousand two hundred and ninety-first.

Wherefore we command you that ye cause the same to be recorded in your chronicles, for a perpetual memorial of the transaction. Witness, Master William of March, our treasurer. At Westminster, the ninth day of July, the nineteenth year of our reign, by a writ of Privy Seal.

Nat. MSS Scot., ii, No. v ; the second letter appears
separately in vol. i, No. lxxi

The crown was awarded to Balliol on 17 November 1292 ; on 20 November 1292 Balliol swore fealty to Edward I ; and on 26 December 1292, at Newcastle-on-Tyne, Balliol did homage to Edward for his kingdom of Scotland. Edward, moreover, soon showed that he intended to treat Balliol and Scotland as a vassal-king and a vassal-state ; and matters reached a crisis when, in 1294, he demanded Scottish levies for his war with France. Balliol, who had proved to be too weak, was then virtually super-seded by a council consisting of four bishops, four earls and four barons ; and in 1295 a defensive alliance against England was concluded with Philip IV of France.

ABSTRACT OF THE TREATY BETWEEN JOHN BALLIOL AND PHILIP OF FRANCE, 1295

The treaty was made at Paris on 23 October 1295. On 24 February following, Balliol confirmed it, when, in addition to several prelates and barons, the communities of the burghs of Aberdeen, Perth, Stirling, Edinburgh, Roxburgh and Berwick appended their seals ' in token of their consent and approval.'

It was agreed between John Balliol and Philip the Fair that Edward Balliol, eldest son of King John, should marry the eldest daughter of Charles, count of Valois and Anjou, Philip's brother. Her dowry was to be 25,000 *petits livres Tournois* and her portion £1,500 sterling annually from the lands of Bailleul, Dampierre, Helicourt and Hornoi in France and the lands of Lanark, Cadzow, Maudisley, Cunningham and Haddington and the castle of Dundee, in Scotland.

In view of the operations being conducted by Edward I against Philip, it was agreed that ' in order that the foresaid injurious efforts may the more conveniently be repressed and that the said king [Edward] be the more quickly compelled to withdraw from his perverse and hostile incursions . . ., the said king of Scots shall take care to begin and continue war against the king of England at his own cost and expense with all his power and with all the power of his subjects and of his kingdom, as often as it be opportune, while we [Philip] prosecute and carry on the war which has been begun. . . . The prelates of Scotland, as far as it be lawful to them, with the earls, barons and other nobles and also the *universitates ac communitates villarum* [1], shall make war against the said king of England in the

---

[1] The burghs

same manner as is above expressed, with all their strength.
. . . The prelates, earls, barons and other nobles and also
the *universitates communitatesque notabiles* of Scotland shall
direct to us as soon as may be their letters patent hereon
fortified with their seals.

'It was also agreed . . . that if it happen the foresaid
king of England to invade . . . the kingdom of Scotland
by himself or by another, after war has been begun by the
king of Scots at our request, or after this present agreement
and treaty has been entered upon between us . . ., we,
provided we be forewarned thereof on the part of the same
king of Scots within a suitable time, shall give him help by
occupying the said king of England in other parts, so that
he shall thus be distracted from beginning the foresaid
invasion. . . . If, however, the foresaid king of England
personally leaves his land of England or goes out of it
with a notable number of infantry or cavalry while war
lasts between him and us, . . . then especially the said king
of Scotland with all his power shall see to it that he invades
the land of England as widely and as deeply as he can,'
attacking by every kind of military operation.

It was also agreed that the king of France ' will refuse to
enter upon peace or truce or to come to an agreement
concerning the war which the said king of Scots and his
successors may be making against the oft-said king of
England on our behalf . . ., or if, by occasion of the
agreement and treaty entered upon, the said king of Scots
has already made the abovesaid war, or the king of England
against him, by reason of any of the premises. Nor will
[the king of France] make an agreement about our own
said war—unless with [the Scots'] inclusion in the peace or
truce which we make about the said wars ; and he himself
[the king of Scots] shall not likewise be able to make peace
or truce about all the abovesaid wars without us.'

A.P.S., i, 451–3 (partly from an incomplete original and
partly from the French archives)

BALLIOL'S SURRENDER AND THE RISING OF WALLACE

On 5 April 1296 Balliol renounced his fealty and homage to
Edward I (at Berwick : Rymer, *Foedera*, i, 836-7) ; and Edward,
to secure ' his fief of Scotland,' soon captured the castles of
Roxburgh, Edinburgh and Stirling, after heavily defeating a
Scottish army at Dunbar. On 10 July 1296, in the churchyard of
Stracathro, Balliol surrendered himself, his kingdom of Scotland,
his people and all their goods to Edward (Stevenson, *Documents*,
ii, 61).

But, early in 1297, William Wallace and Andrew Murray
raised the people against the English occupation of their country
and the English army was so heavily defeated at the battle of
Stirling Bridge (11 September 1297) that Wallace and Murray
felt justified in sending the following letter to Lübeck and Hamburg
in which they announced that the kingdom of Scotland had been
' recovered by war from the power of the English.'

*Letter from Andrew Murray and William Wallace to
Lübeck and Hamburg, 1297*

Andrew of Moray and William Wallace, leaders of the
army of the kingdom of Scotland, and the community of
the same kingdom, to the prudent and discreet men, their
beloved friends the mayors and commons of Lübeck and
of Hamburg, greeting and continual increase of sincere
affection. It has been announced to us by trustworthy
merchants of the said kingdom of Scotland that you, of
your own grace and not out of regard for our deserts, are
considerate, helpful and favourable in all causes and
affairs touching us and our merchants ; and therefore we
are the more bound to you to give you our thanks and a
worthy recompense whereto we willingly engage ourselves
to you, beseeching you that you cause it to be proclaimed
among your merchants that they may have a safe access to
all ports of the kingdom of Scotland with their merchandise,
because the kingdom of Scotland, thanks be to God, is

recovered by war from the power of the English. Farewell. Given at Badsingtona (Haddington) in Scotland, 11 October 1297.

We ask you, moreover, that you deign to promote the business of John Burnet and John Frere, our merchants, as you may wish us to promote the business of your merchants. Farewell. Given as above.

Documents illustrative of Sir William Wallace
(Maitland Club, 1841), No. xv

LETTER FROM THE SCOTS IN FRANCE TO THE GUARDIAN
OF SCOTLAND, 25 MAY 1303

Despite the clauses in the treaty of 1295, whereby Scotland and France both bound themselves against the making of a separate peace, Philip IV, on 23 May 1303, sealed a treaty of perpetual peace and friendship with England (Treaty of Paris). The Scottish ambassadors, then in France for the purpose of securing more effective co-operation against a common enemy, found themselves virtually prisoners ; but their letter, sent to Scotland two days later, is remarkable for its courage and inspiration.

To the venerable and discreet men, their beloved friends in Christ the lords John Comyn, Guardian of the kingdom of Scotland, the prelates, earls, barons and the rest of the faithful of the community of the same realm,—W[illiam de Lamberton] and M[atthew de Crambeth], by divine mercy humble ministers of the churches of St Andrews and Dunkeld, John, earl of Buchan, James, the Steward of Scotland, John de Soules, Ingram de Umfraville and William de Balliol, knights, greeting and triumph over enemies, with the spirit of consolation. Lest you be uninformed of the events of these days in the kingdom of France, we notify you by the tenor of the presents that a final peace was made and sworn between the kings of France and England on Tuesday next after the feast of the Ascension [23 May], and on the same day it was

ordained by the king of France and his council that solemn
messengers, namely the bishop of Amiens, Magnus, prior
of the hospital in France, and Master John de Pochiaco,
should be sent forthwith to the foresaid king of England
to draw him back from the war of Scotland and for the
sake of securing an armistice for you until a certain time,
so that in the meantime the foresaid kings may personally
convene in France and hold treaty with each other, wherein
the king of France shall make our peace useful for our
realm [of Scotland] as the same king most firmly promised
us ; and the reason why his peace should go before ours
is because it appeared by the counsel as well of the king
of France as of the king of England (following on weighty
deliberation thereon), that after concord and friendship
have been contracted between them, our peace may be the
more quickly, easily and usefully arrived at ; therefore the
king of France wished to make peace with the king of
England so that he could thereby arrive more quickly at
our peace ; and therefore be you not disturbed or troubled
in anything if the English tell you that peace has been
made between the kings to the exclusion of the Scots,
because the reason why it has been so done is expressed
above. Wherefore we beg and soundly advise you that
you be full of courage, and if the said king of England
be willing to consent to the armistice—as he will consent,
as we firmly hope—that you likewise consent according to
the form which the foresaid envoys of the king of France
will send you by one of us who shall be known to you,
whom we shall send to you in company with the said
envoys—even although it may chance that this armistice
will be harmful to some in that, in the meantime, they will
lack their lands—since it is expedient that some sustain
slight harm for a short time in order that afterwards
greater benefit may ensue. If, however, the said king of
England be so obdurate, in the manner of Pharaoh, that
he will not consent to the truce, but continue the war with
you, by the mercy of Jesus Christ manfully and as one man
defend yourselves, so that by your manly defence you may

conquer with the help of God, or at least until you receive from us other encouragement. Do not marvel that none of us comes to you at present, for we should gladly all come, but the king of France has not allowed that any of us leave until we may carry with us the outcome of the negotiations ; when that is achieved, howsoever it be, we shall come to you, notwithstanding any danger by land or sea ; and therefore, for God's sake, in no way despair, but if you have ever done manfully, do only more manfully, because according to Holy Writ ' though he runs swiftly he runs in vain who fails ere he reach the mark ' ; and if you knew how much honour has come to you throughout many regions of the globe from your last fight against the English, you would greatly rejoice. You are to know for certain that in those matters which make for the speed of the negotiations we shall, so far as in us lies, omit nothing relating thereto—just as we have hitherto, God knows, omitted nothing. The envoys of the king of France who are to come to the king of England shall have power not only to make an armistice but also to treat of final peace with the king of England, just as was said to us by the counsel of the king of France, to shorten the negotiations ; therefore, if they would treat with you, keep yourselves discreetly in this same treaty to the best of your ability, lest you be deceived by the fraud of adversaries. . . . If therefore the envoys of the king of France come to you, you are to receive them honourably for your honour and that of the kingdom. At Paris, viii Kal. Junii.

A.P.S., i, 454–5 (from the original letter)

LETTER OF THE MAGNATES OF SCOTLAND TO THE KING OF FRANCE, 16 MARCH 1308/9

The intercession on behalf of Scotland promised by Philip IV, if made, failed in its purpose. Edward I vigorously prosecuted the war against Scotland ; but in 1306 Scotland found a new leader in Robert Bruce. There is no record evidence for Bruce's assumption of the crown, but his reign is dated from 27 March 1306 ; and descriptions of his ' coronation ' at Scone are to be found in the chronicles.[1] After initial setbacks (and also after the death of Edward I on 7 July 1307) Bruce and his supporters gained important successes in almost every part of Scotland. These successes, and the growing strength of his following, enabled Bruce to hold his first parliament, at St Andrews, on 16 March 1308/9. From this parliament a letter was addressed to the king of France setting out in explicit terms that Bruce was not only king of Scotland but was recognised as such by the prelates, magnates and community of the whole kingdom. The names in the opening recital are in themselves evidence of the widespread support for Bruce's cause.

To the most Christian and victorious prince and lord the worshipful lord Philip, by the grace of God illustrious king of the French—William, earl of Ross, Malcolm, earl of Lennox, William [earl of Suther]land, the communities of the earldoms of Fife, Menteith, Mar, Buchan and Caithness (the heirs of which are in ward), the communities also of the other earldoms of the whole kingdom of Scotland [. . . D]unbar [2], Edward Bruce, lord of Galloway, James the Steward of Scotland, Alexander of Argyll, Donald of Islay, John of Menteith, Hugh, son and heir of the earl [of . . .] [2], Gilbert Hay, Constable of Scotland, Robert Keith, Marischal of Scotland, Thomas Randolph, lord of Nithsdale, James, lord of Douglas, Alexander Lindsay, Alexander D[. . .], William Wiseman, David Berkeley, Robert Boyd, the barons also of the whole of Argyll and the Isles [Ynchegallya] and the inhabitants of the whole kingdom of Scotland acknowledging the faith of the lord Robert, by the grace of God king of Scotland, [. . .] greeting. Your message, shown to us in writing and fully understood in a full parliament of our lord the king of Scotland lately held with solemnity at the city

[1] See Dunbar, *Scottish Kings*, 129 , *n.* 13
[2] These, and the other gaps, are due to the state of the original manuscript, which is damaged.

of St Andrews, impressed our minds and [. . .] joy and
devotion. We indeed give careful regard to a kingly mind
open to devotion to take up the affairs of the holy land,
for the furtherance of which Christians ought rightly to
direct their minds and most warmly incline their hearts
[. . .] we see it contained that royal gratitude reflects
on and brings back to mind the alliances formerly existing
and maintained between the kingdoms of France and
Scotland and the losses, sufferings and trials which the
inhabitants of the kingdom [. . .] have hitherto so much
endured. Our minds are cheered, above all, by the
extraordinary and peculiar affection which, by the same
message, you say you have for the person of lord Robert,
by the grace of God our lord king, who has been raised
up as our leader and prince by right and truth and by the
justice and grace of the King of Kings. We, therefore,
heartily considering the foregoing as we are obliged,
[? commend] your royal devotion for the affairs of the
holy land . . . and for the regard you have towards our
lord king, and we return all the thanks we can to your royal
majesty for the restoration of the liberties and rights of the
kingdom of Scotland [. . .], praying that, in the bowels
of mercy of Jesus Christ, your majesty [. . .] the devotion
which, with God's guidance, you have conceived in your
mind with regard to all the foregoing, with holy desire and
careful affection, and with a salutary end [. . .] and that
your royal majesty may deign to notice, with pious mind,
that in the exaltation of Christian princes the name of
Christ is extolled and the Catholic faith strengthened.
If, therefore, the estate of our lord [. . .] to be we say
indivisibly, be uplifted by the grace of your excellency,
and the kingdom of Scotland restored to its original liberty,
the storms of war extinguished, the security of peace
granted, [. . .] the purpose of your desire in divine service
and your help, your highness may have at power not only
our lord the king foresaid but also the inhabitants of his
realm. And that the foregoing [. . .] be patent we have
thought fit openly to direct these letters, sealed with our

seals, to your highness. Written and given at the city of St Andrews in Scotland the 16th day of March the year of grace 1308 and the third year of our lord King Robert.

A.P.S., i, 459 (from the original deed)

DECLARATION OF THE CLERGY IN FAVOUR OF KING ROBERT THE BRUCE, 24 FEBRUARY 1309/10 [1]

Further recognition soon came to Robert I ; and the clergy of Scotland, possibly in February 1310, made the following stirring declaration in his favour :

To all the faithful in Christ to whose knowledge the present writing shall come, the Bishops, Abbots, Priors, and the rest of the Clergy in the Kingdom of Scotland greeting in the Author of Salvation. Be it known to you all that when between the Lord John de Balliol, lately in fact raised to be King of Scotland by the King of England, and the deceased Lord Robert de Brus of worthy memory, grandfather of the Lord Robert the King who now is, a ground of dispute had arisen which of them, to wit, was nearest by right of blood to inherit and reign over the Scottish people ; the faithful people without doubt always held, as from their predecessors and ancestors they had learned and believed to be true, that the said Lord Robert, the grandfather, after the death of King Alexander and his granddaughter, the daughter of the King of Norway, was the true heir, and ought, in preference to all others, to be advanced to the government of the kingdom, although the enemy of the human race sowing tares, by the various machinations and plots of his rivals, which it would be tedious to narrate at length, the thing has turned contrariwise ; on account of whose overthrow, and the want of kingly authority, heavy calamities have thenceforth resulted to the Kingdom of Scotland and its inhabitants, as

---

[1] There are difficulties about accepting this date, as Dundee was in English hands at that time (*Scot. Hist. Rev.*, xxiii, 284).

experience, the mistress of events, hitherto often repeated, has manifestly declared. The people, therefore, and commons of the foresaid Kingdom of Scotland, worn out by the stings of many tribulations, seeing the said Lord John, by the King of England, on various pretexts, taken, imprisoned, stripped of his kingdom and people, and the Kingdom of Scotland by him also ruined and reduced to slavery, laid waste by a mighty depopulation, and overwhelmed by the bitterness of frequent grief, desolated from the want of right government, exposed to every danger, and given up to the spoiler, and the people stripped of their goods, tortured by wars, led captive, bound, and imprisoned ; by immense massacres of the innocent, and by continual conflagrations, oppressed, subjugated and enslaved, and on the brink of total ruin, unless by divine guidance steps should very quickly be taken for the restoration and government of the kingdom thus marred and desolated : by the providence of the Supreme King, under whose government kings rule and princes bear sway, being no longer able to bear so many and so great heavy losses of things and persons more bitter than death, often happening for want of a captain and faithful leader, with divine sanction agreed upon the said Lord Robert, the King who now is, in whom the rights of his father and grandfather to the foresaid kingdom, in the judgment of the people, still exist and flourish entire ; and with the concurrence and consent of the said people he was chosen to be King, that he might reform the deformities of the kingdom, correct what required correction, and direct what needed direction ; and having been by their authority set over the kingdom, he was solemnly made King of Scots, and with him the faithful people of the kingdom will live and die as with one who, possessing the right of blood, and endowed with the other cardinal virtues, is fitted to rule, and worthy of the name of King and the honour of the kingdom, since, by the grace of the Saviour, by repelling injustice, he has by the sword restored the realm thus deformed and ruined, as many former princes and kings of the Scots had by the sword restored, acquired, and held the said kingdom when often ruined in times bygone, as is more fully contained in the ancient glorious histories of the Scots, and as the warlike toils of the Picts against the Britons and of the Scots against the Picts, expelled from the kingdom, with many others anciently routed, subdued and expelled by the sword, manifestly testify ; and if any one on the contrary claim right to the foresaid kingdom in virtue of letters in time past, sealed and containing the consent of the people and the commons, know ye that all this took place in fact by force and violence which could not at the time be resisted, and through multiplied fears, bodily tortures, and various terrors, enough to confound the senses and distract the minds of perfect men and fall on the sted-fast. We, therefore, the Bishops, Abbots, Priors and the rest of the Clergy, aforesaid, knowing that the premises are based on truth, and cordially approving the same, have made due fealty to our said Lord Robert, the illustrious King of Scotland, and we acknowledge, and by the tenor of these presents publicly declare, that the same ought to be rendered to him and his heirs by our successors for ever ; and in sign of testimony and approbation of all the foregoing, not compelled by force, induced by fraud, or falling through error, but of pure and lasting and spontaneous free will, have caused our seals to be affixed to this writing. Given in the General Council of Scotland, celebrated in the Church of the Friars Minor of Dundee, the twenty-fourth day of the month of February, in the year of the Lord one thousand three hundred and nine, and in the year of the said reign the fourth.

Nat. MSS Scot., ii, No. xvii ; *A.P.S.*, i, 460
(from the original deed)

THE STATUTE OF CAMBUSKENNETH, 6 NOVEMBER 1314

Immediately following the victory at Bannockburn a parliament at Cambuskenneth forfeited all those who had fought on the side of England and who had not come ' into the faith and peace ' of Robert I. This was to have its repercussions early in the reign of David II when the ' Disinherited ' were able to rally many of the forfeited to their side.

In a parliament held in the monastery of Cambuskenneth by a most excellent prince Lord Robert, by the grace of God illustrious king of Scots, it was agreed, finally adjudged and decided hereon with the counsel and assent of the bishops and the rest of the prelates, earls, barons and other nobles of the kingdom of Scotland, and also of the whole community of the kingdom foresaid, that all who died in war, or elsewhere, contrary to the faith and peace of the said lord king, or who on the said day had not come into his peace and faith (although oft-times called and lawfully awaited), be disinherited for ever of their lands and tenements and of all their other estate within the kingdom of Scotland, and be held, besides, as enemies of the king and kingdom, deprived of all vindication of heritable right or of any other right hereafter for themselves and their heirs forever. In perpetual memory, evidence and proof, therefore, of this judgment and statute, the seals of the bishops and other prelates and of the earls, barons and the rest of the nobles of the said realm are appended to the present ordinance, judgment and statute.

A.P.S., i, 464 (from the original instrument)

Numerous instances of new grants of forfeited lands are to be found in *R.M.S.*, i, Nos. 1–96.

THE SETTLEMENT OF THE SUCCESSION, 1315, 1318

Meantime the heir to the crown was Marjorie, daughter of Robert I by his first wife Isabella of Mar ; and, in the difficult times through which the kingdom was passing, the magnates felt that if the king were to die it was essential that he should be succeeded on the throne by a man ' vigorous and skilled in warfare.' Accordingly, in an assembly at Ayr, on 27 April 1315, it was agreed that if Robert I died without leaving a surviving son, his brother, Edward Bruce, *tanquam vir strenuus et in actibus bellicis expertus*, and his heirs male should succeed to the Crown.

Edward Bruce, however, was killed in Ireland, in October 1318, leaving no lawful heir, and thus the settlement of 1315 fell to the ground. Accordingly, in December 1318, a parliament held at Scone declared Robert, the only son of Marjorie Bruce and Walter the High Steward, to be heir to the Crown if Robert Bruce had no male issue.

But David, son of Robert Bruce, was born in March 1324 ; he succeeded as David II on 7 June 1329 ; but when he died without issue in February 1371 he was succeeded, in virtue of this settlement, by Robert, only son of Marjorie Bruce, as Robert II, the first of the Stewart kings.

The texts of these decisions are taken from Sir James Balfour's transcripts as reprinted in the *Acts of the Parliaments*. There is no extant official record of the decisions ; but there is no reason to doubt these versions. The lists of the seals, however, as given in Balfour's transcripts, are possibly less trustworthy.

At Ayr, 27 April 1315

In the year 1315 on the [27 April], at Ayr, in the parish church of that place, the bishops, abbots, priors, deans, archdeacons and the rest of the prelates of the churches, the earls, barons, knights and the rest of the community of the kingdom of Scotland, cleric and lay, gathered together to treat, discuss and ordain upon the state, defence and permanent security of the kingdom of Scotland, unanimously agreed and ordained in the following manner :

1 That each and all of them, cleric and lay, would obey as their king and liege lord against all mortals and faithfully support in all things the magnificent prince their liege lord, Lord Robert, by the grace of God illustrious king of Scotland, now reigning, and the heirs male of his body lawfully to be begotten.

2 They also ordained with the consent of the said lord king and of his daughter Marjorie, heir apparent, on the day of the present ordinance, that if it happened (which God forbid) that the said lord king closed the last day of his life without any surviving male heir begotten of his body, the noble man Lord Edward de Brus, brother of the king, as a vigorous man and as most highly skilled in warfare for the defence of the right and liberty of the kingdom of Scotland, and the heirs male of his body to be lawfully begotten, shall succeed the said lord king in the kingdom. And all the aforesaid clergy and laymen will obey them in all things as king and lord in succession as is expressed above in relation to the person of the lord king and his heirs.

3 They ordained with the consent of the said king and of the said Lord Edward, his brother, that in the absence of lawful descendants of the said Lord Edward and his heirs male of his body (which God forbid) the succession of the said kingdom of Scotland shall revert to the above-mentioned Marjorie, whom failing to the nearest heir lineally descended from the body of King Robert, without challenge of any man, until, with the consent of the said lord king or, whom failing (which God forbid), with the consent of the greater part of the community of the kingdom, the said Marjorie shall be joined in marriage.

4 They ordained that if the aforesaid lord king should die, leaving as heir male a minor, or the said Lord Edward, his brother, should die in a like manner, . . . the noble man Lord Thomas Randolph, earl of Moray, shall have guardianship of the heir and the kingdom until such time as it shall appear to the community of the realm, or to the greater part thereof, that the heir himself is able to undertake the rule of his realm.

5 They moreover ordained that if the said Marjorie shall die in widowhood leaving her heir a minor in the manner above expressed, the said earl shall have guardianship of the heir and the kingdom as is expressed above in the cases of the heirs of the lord king and his brother, if the said earl shall assent thereto. If the said Marjorie shall die

leaving no heir of her body and if no heir of King Robert's body is surviving (which God forbid), the said earl shall have guardianship of the kingdom until he can conveniently convene the prelates, earls, barons and others of the community of the realm to ordain and discuss concerning the lawful succession and government of the kingdom.

A.P.S., i, 464–5

At Scone, 3 December 1318

It was ordained and by the unanimous consent of each and all [of the aforesaid prelates, earls, barons and the rest of the community of the kingdom] it was agreed that if if happen (which God forbid) that the lord king should close his last day with no male heir lawfully begotten of his body surviving, Robert, son of the Lady Marjorie of good memory, daughter of the lord king, lawfully begotten of the noble man Lord Walter, Steward of Scotland, her husband, shall fully succeed the same lord king in his kingdom as his nearest lawful heir : whom all the above shall obey in all things and faithfully support, as was above expressed of the person of the lord king.

The lord king, with the unanimous consent of one and all of the community, has assigned the wardship or care of the said Robert, or of other heir begotten of the body of the lord king, together with the custody of the whole kingdom and people, if at the time of the decease of the lord king the heir shall be of minor age, to the noble man Lord Thomas Randolph, earl of Moray and lord of Man ; and if, in the meantime, the said earl shall have chanced to die (which God forbid), to the noble man Lord James of Douglas ; until such time as it shall seem to the community of the realm, or to the greater and wiser part thereof, that the said Robert, or other heir of the lord king, as above expressed, is able himself to take over the rule of the kingdom and the people.

A.P.S., i, 465

THE LETTER OF THE SCOTTISH BARONS TO THE POPE, 1320
(The Declaration of Arbroath)

Although Bannockburn had been fought and won, and although the succession to the Crown had been settled, England refused to admit the independence of Scotland, and the pope, John XXII, refused to recognise Bruce as king. Moreover, at the instance of Edward II, the pope cited four of the Scottish bishops to answer at Avignon, and sent two legates to publish a sentence of excommunication against Bruce and to absolve the people from their obedience to him if he still contumaciously refused to make peace with England.

The answer was the ' Letter of the Barons,' sealed at Arbroath on 6 April 1320, ' in haste to forestall the legates ' who had reached Berwick on 17 March. The letter is an appeal for justice, and a declaration on behalf of Bruce ; but it is also a manifesto of a united nation, determined to resist English aggression and to oust even Bruce should he show any sign of weakening in the cause.

Although the letter ran in the names of the barons, and was sealed only by the barons, there is no doubt that it had the full support of the church ; it was almost certainly drafted by Bernard de Linton, abbot of Arbroath, Bruce's chancellor.

To the most holy father and lord in Christ the lord John, by divine providence supreme pontiff of the holy Roman and universal church, his humble and devoted sons Duncan, earl of Fife, Thomas Randolph, earl of Moray, lord of Man and Annandale, Patrick of Dunbar, earl of March, Malise, earl of Strathearn, Malcolm, earl of Lennox, William, earl of Ross, Magnus, earl of Caithness and Orkney, William, earl of Sutherland, Walter, Steward of Scotland, William of Soulis, Butler of Scotland, James, lord of Douglas, Roger Moubray, David, lord of Brechin, David Graham, Ingram de Umfraville, John Menteith, guardian of the earldom of Menteith, Alexander Fraser, Gilbert Hay, Constable of Scotland, Robert Keith, Marischal of Scotland, Henry St Clair, John Graham, David Lindsay, William Oliphant,

Patrick Graham, John Fenton, William Abernethy, David Wemyss, William Muschett, Fergus of Ardrossan, Eustace Maxwell, William Ramsay, William Mowat, Alan Moray, Donald Campbell, John Cambrun, Reginald le Chene, Alexander Seton, Andrew Leslie and Alexander Straton and the rest of the barons and freeholders and the whole community of the realm of Scotland, all manner of filial reverence with devoted kisses of your blessed feet.

Most holy father and lord, we know, and we learn from the deeds and records of the men of old, that among peoples of renown our Scottish people have been distinguished by many tributes to their fame. Passing from Greater Scythia over the Tyrrhenian Sea and by the pillars of Hercules, abiding for long courses of time in Spain among the fiercest of warriors, by none how barbaric soever could they be anywhere brought under the yoke. And thence coming, twelve hundred years after the setting forth of the people of Israel, they won for themselves by victory after victory and travail upon travail the abodes in the west which now they hold, the Britons expelled, the Picts utterly destroyed, assailed again and again by Norseman, Dane and Angle ; and this their home, as the histories of the ancients bear witness, they have kept evermore free from any servitude. Within their realm have reigned one hundred and thirteen kings of native royal stock, never an alien upon the throne. Their noble qualities and worth, were there nought else to show, shine forth for all to see in that the King of Kings and our Lord Jesus Christ after His passion and resurrection called these very men, dwelling at the limit of the world, almost the first to His most holy faith, nor would have them confirmed therein through any but the first of His apostles by calling albeit in rank second or third, to wit Andrew the Meek, brother of the Blessed Peter, whom He chose to be ever more their leader and patron.

The holy fathers your predecessors, mindful and careful hereof, fortified the same kingdom and people, as the peculiar possession of St Peter's brother, with many favours and many a privilege, in so much that our folk lived under their protection free and undisturbed, until the masterful prince Edward, king of the English, father of him who reigns now, came in the guise of a friend and an ally with a hostile intent against our realm when it lacked a head, against a people who had no thought of ill or fraud, unused to the assaults of war. The wrongs he did among them, slaughter, violence, pillage, burning, prelates imprisoned, monasteries given to the flames, the inmates despoiled and slain, and these not all his lawless deeds, sparing neither age, sex, order of religion nor priesthood, only he who saw and suffered might recount or comprehend.

From these unnumbered ills, with the aid of Him who heals the wounded and makes whole, we have been delivered by the strong arm of our prince and king, our lord Sir Robert, who, that he might free his people and his heritage from the hands of foes, a second Maccabeus as it were or a Joshua, endured cheerfully toil and weariness, hunger and peril. And he it is that by the providence of God, by rightful succession after our laws and customs, the which we will maintain even unto death, and by the dutiful consent and assent of every one of us, has been made our prince and king. Unto him, as the man through whom salvation has been wrought in our people, we are bound both of right and by his service rendered, and are resolved in whatever fortune to cleave, for the preservation of our liberty. Were he to abandon the enterprise begun, choosing to subject us or our kingdom to the king of the English or to the English people, we would strive to thrust him out forthwith as our enemy and the subverter of right, his own and ours, and take for our king another who would suffice for our defence ; for so long as an hundred remain alive we are minded never a whit to bow beneath the yoke of English dominion. It is not for glory, riches or honours that we fight : it is for liberty alone, the liberty which no good man relinquishes but with his life.

Wherefore it is, revered Father and Lord, that we do pray your Holiness most fervently with suppliant hearts and voices : bethink you in all sincerity and justice that with Him whose vice-gerent you are upon the earth there is no balancing of persons, no distinction of Jew and Greek, Scot or Englishman : look with a father's eye upon the sorrow and distress brought by the English upon us and on the church of God : be pleased to admonish and exhort the king of the English, whom it behoves to be content with what he has, seeing that of old England was wont to suffice seven kings or more, to leave us Scots in peace, dwelling in our poor Scotia, beyond which lies no place of habitation, seeking nothing but our own : to whom for the sake of peace we are willing to render in very deed all that our state enables us to offer. For so to do, Holy Father, is of concern for you who behold their own ill deeds bring upon Christians the rage of the heathen, and the bounds of Christendom contract from day to day. How grievously must the memory of your Holiness be impaired if, as God forbid, the church in any part thereof within your time suffer eclipse or offence—that you cannot but have seen. Let your Holiness therefore stir up Christian princes who have no ground but an excuse and feign that they cannot go to the succour of the Holy Land because of the wars they are waging with their neighbours : whereof the truer reason is that in the conquest of the weaker on their borders they count their profit readier and resistance feebler. Nay, how gladly would our king and we go thither, did the king of the English but leave us in peace, He from whom nought is hidden knows right well. To the Vicar of Christ and to all Christendom we declare it and bear our testimony. If your Holiness take us not at our word, putting too easy a faith in what the English say, or haply cease not to favour them and we be confounded, the lives cut off, the souls sped, all the evil to be done by them in us and by us in them, we believe that the Most High must lay to your account. Wherefore we are and shall be in that wherein we are bound as sons of obedience to you His vicar ready to fulfil your pleasure in all things ; and to Him as King and Judge supreme we commit the defence of our cause, casting all our care upon Him, with constant hope that He will strengthen our manhood and bring our foes to nought.

May the Most High keep your Holiness in health of mind and body to serve His Holy Church for many a day.

Given at the monastery of Abirbrothoc in Scotland the sixth day of April in the year of grace one thousand three hundred and twenty in the fifteenth year of our aforesaid king.

A.P.S., i, 474–5

Latin text in *Scotichronicon*, lib. xiii, caps. 2–3 and in *Nat. MSS Scot.*, ii, No. xxiv. Translations in *Nat. MSS*, in R. K. Hannay, *The barons of Scotland to Pope John XXII in 1320* [1936], and in Lord Cooper, *Supra Crepidam* [1951]. See also *S.H.R.*, xxvi, 75–8 ; xxix, 119–20.

TREATY OF CORBEUIL, 1326

At Corbeuil in April 1326 an agreement was made between Charles IV of France and Robert I of Scotland against the King of England, binding on their successors. No official copy of the agreement is extant, but a transcript is contained in the ' Black Book ' preserved in H.M. Register House. The essential clauses in the agreement were—

That the kings of France, their heirs and successors, their realm and whole community, are obliged and bound to the said king of Scotland, his heirs and successors kings of Scotland, his realm and whole community, in good faith as loyal allies that every time when they shall have to give aid or counsel in time of peace or war against the king of England, his heirs and successors kings of England and his subjects, the kings of France will aid and counsel the kings of Scotland to the best of their power as loyal allies and if they, their heirs and successors kings of France [etc.] conclude peace or make truces with the king of England [etc.] the king of Scotland [etc.] shall be excepted so that that peace or truce shall be null if war arises between the aforesaid kings of Scotland and England. And if the king of Scotland [etc.] conclude peace or make truces with the king of England [etc.] the kings of France [etc.] shall be excepted so that that peace or truce shall be null if war breaks out between the king of France and the said king of England. And if war arises between the king of France and the king of England, the said kings of Scotland [etc.] are obliged to the king of France and his heirs [etc.] to make war on the king of England to the utmost of their power, any truce between the said kings of Scotland and England, taken or pending in any manner, to be at an end.

A.P.S., xii, 5

THE TREATY OF EDINBURGH-NORTHAMPTON, 1328

In 1323 England and Scotland concluded a truce which was to last till 1336. It was confirmed when Edward III succeeded Edward II at the beginning of 1327 ; but in the summer of that year there was a Scottish raid into England, and an attempt at retaliation proved so futile that the English government (in the hands of Isabella, the Queen Mother, and her paramour Mortimer) decided to open negotiations for peace. Parleys at Newcastle in November 1327 were followed in February 1328 by discussions at York, when the English evidently decided to acknowledge Bruce as king and Scotland as free from subjection, whereby a treaty could be entered into with Scotland as an independent nation. Scottish representatives had gone to York, but proceedings there were adjourned to allow of the visit to Edinburgh of an influential English delegation, authorised to negotiate a final peace and to arrange the marriage of David Bruce with the English princess Joanna. Discussions took place in a chamber within the walls of the abbey of Holyrood, where Bruce lay, and agreement was reached on 17 March 1327/8. King Edward's confirmation was dated at Northampton on 4 May.

The ' treaty ' was contained in several documents :

(1) Two bipartite indentures, one in French and one in Latin. The Scottish half of the French indenture is preserved in the Register House, and a translation of excerpts from it is given below.

(2) Two notarial instruments binding Bruce to meet his

obligation to pay £20,000 to England—an obligation alluded to in the indentures.

(3) Letters patent whereby Bruce undertook to assign an annual income to Joanna.

Be it known to all those who shall see these letters that on the seventeenth day of March [1327/8] the things under-written were treated and accorded between the right excellent prince Robert, by the grace of God king of Scotland, on the one part, and the honourable fathers in God Henry, by the permission of God bishop of Lincoln, William, by the same permission bishop of Norwich, Henry de Percy, William la Zouche of Assheby and Geoffrey Lescrope, messengers and procurators by special commission of [Edward III] to treat of a final peace, and to confirm and assure the said peace, between the said king of England and the aforesaid king of Scotland, upon wars moved between the kingdoms of England and Scotland, on the other part, in manner underwritten, that is to say :

Firstly, that good peace, final and perpetual, be between the said kings, their heirs and successors, and their kingdoms and lands, and between their subjects and peoples, on the one part and the other, in the form which follows—

And for the assurance and confirming of this peace it is treated and accorded that a marriage be made, at the earliest that it can be duly made, between David, eldest son and heir of the said king of Scotland, and Joan, sister of the foresaid king of England, who as yet are of so tender age that they cannot make contract of matrimony ; and, for the assurance of the said marriage, an oath is made on the souls of the said kings, by the persons above named, and of the prelates and other great men of the kingdom of Scotland.

And that the foresaid king of Scotland shall give and assign to the said Joan, in places suitable in his kingdom of Scotland, £2,000 of land and of rent by year. . . .

And, if it happen that God does His will of the said Joan before the said marriage be completed or accom-plished, that then the said king of England, his heirs or his successors, have the marriage of the said David for another nearest and most suitable of their blood, and that she to whom he shall be married have the said £2,000 of land. . . .

And, if it happen that God does His will of the said David before the said marriage be completed or accomplished, that then the said king of England . . . have the marriage of the next heir male of the foresaid king of Scotland for the said Joan. . . .

Item, it is treated and accorded that the said kings, their heirs and successors, shall be good friends and loyal allies, and that the one shall aid the other in suitable manner as good allies : saving on the part of the king of Scotland the alliance made between him and the king of France. But if it happen that the said king of Scotland . . . by reason of the said alliance or for any other cause whatever make war upon the said king of England, . . . that the said king of England . . . may make war on the aforesaid king of Scotland. . . .

Item, it is treated and accorded that if any levy war in Ireland against the said king of England, . . . the foresaid king of Scotland . . . shall not assist the said enemies of the said king of England ; also . . . that if any levy war against the foresaid king of Scotland . . . in the Isle of Man or in the other islands of Scotland, the said king of England . . . shall not assist the said enemies.

Item, . . . that all writs, obligations, instruments and other muniments touching the subjection of the people or of the land of Scotland to the king of England, the which are annulled and voided by the letters of the said king of England, and all other instruments and privileges touching the freedom of Scotland that can be found in good faith with the king of England, be given up and restored to the foresaid king of Scotland at the earliest that they can well be, according as they shall be found, so that of this delivery there be made an indenture of each writ, obligation, instrument and muniment that shall be delivered. . . .

Item, . . . that the said king of England shall assist in good faith that the processes, if any are made in the Court of Rome and elsewhere by the authority of our Holy Father the Pope against the said king of Scotland, his realm and his subjects, cleric or lay, be dismissed, with their effect ; and this to do and accomplish he shall send his special letters of prayer to the pope and the cardinals.

Item, . . . forasmuch as the said king of Scotland, the prelates and other great men of his realm, are bound to the said king of England in £20,000 sterling, to be paid in three years at three terms at Tweedmouth, and for this payment so making have submitted themselves to the jurisdiction of the papal *camera* . . ., nevertheless the said messengers and procurators of the king of England in his name will and grant for certain reasons that no execution, condemnation or denunciation be made by any judge of the papal *camera* against the said king of Scotland or the others bound, until the end of two months after each term of the said three terms. . . .

In witness whereof, to one part of this indenture, remaining with the said messengers and procurators, we have caused put our seal. And we the aforesaid messengers and procurators to the other part of the said indenture, remaining with the said king of Scotland, have put our seals. Given at Edinburgh, the 17th day of March, the year of grace [1327/8].

Nat. MSS Scot., ii, No. xxvi

It is to be observed that the treaty, as recorded in extant documents, did not include certain terms sometimes attributed to it :

(1) There is no mention of the Coronation Stone. The record evidence that it may have been intended to return the stone to Scotland is (a) a privy seal writ ordering the abbot of Westminster to hand it over to Isabella (*Rotuli Parliamentorum*, ii, 442) ; and (b) a privy seal writ ordering the sheriffs of London to receive the stone (*Calendar of Plea and Memoranda Rolls of the City of London, 1323–64*, 63). Isabella was at this time about to set forth for Berwick for the marriage of David and Joanna.

(2) There is no trace of a formal agreement on the restoration of the ' Disinherited '—the Anglo-Scottish lords who had taken

the English side and had lost their Scottish estates, though apparently Bruce later agreed to the restoration of Wake, Percy and Beaumont.

(3) There is no trace of an agreement to restore the Black Rood of Scotland, yet evidently it was restored—only to be lost again by David II at Neville's Cross.

> These notes are based on G. L. Stones, ' The English Mission to Edinburgh in 1328,' in *S.H.R.*, xxviii, and ' An Addition to the "Rotuli Scotiae,"' in *S.H.R.*, xxix.

BULL OF POPE JOHN XXII, AUTHORISING THE ANOINTING OF THE KINGS OF SCOTLAND, 13 JUNE 1329

In 1221 Alexander II had unsuccessfully applied to the Pope for coronation by a representative of the Apostolic See. In 1233 he again applied unsuccessfully ; and in 1251, shortly after the accession of Alexander III, Henry III of England petitioned Pope Innocent IV for a mandate to forbid the anointing or coronation of the king of Scots without the consent of the king of England ' whose liegeman the king of Scots was.'

Bruce had been inaugurated as king without the old accustomed rites ; but he had more than justified his kingship. He had, moreover, by the Treaty of Edinburgh-Northampton in 1328, been recognised by England as the independent king of an independent nation. And now, in what were to be the closing months of his reign, he sent ambassadors to the Pope to request that he and his successors might be anointed and crowned by the Bishop of St Andrews. The request was granted in a bull issued by John XXII on 13 June 1329, but Bruce had died six days earlier, at Cardross, on 7 June.

Thus David II was the first Scottish king to be anointed and crowned.

It is important to remember that, by virtue of unction, the sovereign was regarded at this time as ' God's ruler on earth,' and that he became a *mixta persona*, in part a priest and in part a layman.

John, Bishop, servant of the servants of God, to his dearest son in Christ, Robert, illustrious King of Scotland :

Greeting and apostolic benediction. By the Most High, the Eternal King of the heavenly kingdom, through whom all kings reign and princes bear sway, the power of the temporal sword has been given to them for the punishment of evil-doers and the praise of them that do well, that they may judge the peoples in righteousness and in the earth rule the nations placed under their dominion, and that their pleasure may be in the execution of justice and their meditation in the law of uprightness and in the observance of good peace, for the more perfect exercise whereof the said kings, by virtue of the sacred anointing, which according to ancient usage they receive at the hands of the venerable ministers of God, obtain the gift of more special grace, both that they may be strengthened in the prosecution of good government, and, as well in what regards themselves as in things touching their subjects, be governed by a more prudent and sanctified spirit. For powerful on kings is the efficacy of such anointing, insomuch that when Saul was anointed the Spirit of the Lord descended upon him and he was changed into another man ; and upon David, as soon as he was anointed, the Spirit of the Lord was sent down ; to foreshadow also that in kings there ought to be a fulness of the virtues and the complete authority of the temporal dominion, a diadem of honour in circular shape is placed upon the head of the Prince, that from him who has been adorned with such insignia and distinguished by such titles, as from the head, to his subjects as to the members, the example of right living and the rule of moderation may be displayed. With good reason you, as a most devoted son of the Church and a Catholic prince, devoutly regarding the dew of spiritual grace which by such anointing is poured on, are led fervently to desire that the Roman Church, mother and mistress of you and of all the faithful, would vouchsafe the strength of her authority and bestow the protection of the apostolic sanction that, to you and the Catholic princes who shall lawfully succeed you in the foresaid kingdom, such anointing and coronation by the sacred hand of a pontiff may be bestowed ; especially since, as we have learned from the tenor of your petition, both you and your predecessors kings of Scotland have from the most ancient times been wont to receive the insignia of royal dignity from the bishops of St Andrews who were for the time. Wherefore you, by your special ambassadors whom expressly for this purpose you have despatched to the Apostolic See, have humbly supplicated us that we would deign of our special favour to grant by apostolic authority to you, that you and your successors kings of Scotland may receive coronation and anointing with the other symbols of royalty from the bishop of St Andrews who shall be for the time, he being willing and able, but otherwise from another bishop of the kingdom of Scotland. Seeing therefore the devoutness of your sincerity in many ways manifested, and considering that you will study to show yourself so much the more prompt in obedience to the Holy See as you perceive it more propitious and benignant to you, we, yielding a ready assent to your supplications, by the advice of our brethren grant, by the tenor of these presents, that both you and your successors who shall lawfully succeed you in the foresaid kingdom, continuing in devotion to the Roman Church, may receive anointing and the royal crown from the bishop of St Andrews, or if he happen to be unwilling without reasonable cause, or even unable to perform the same, then from the bishop of Glasgow who is or shall be for the time, he having the favour and communion of the Apostolic See, and the said bishop of St Andrews, or, he being unwilling or even unable as aforesaid to perform the same, the said bishop of Glasgow with apostolic authority, bringing with him a becoming number of bishops both for showing respect to the king and reverence to the sacred anointing, shall have power in manner due to anoint you and your successors foresaid, and, by authority aforesaid, to place the royal crown on your and their heads : Saving always however the rights of the Roman Church, and of any other, in all things. We will moreover that the said bishop, who shall perform the premises as aforesaid, receive from the said kings at the time of such anointing and coronation, in our name and in that of the said Roman Church, their bodily oath [1] that they shall endeavour, in good faith according to their power, to exterminate all heretics denounced by the Church from the foresaid kingdom and their other lands and those subject to their authority, and that they shall not presume by themselves or by others to injure or diminish the liberties and immunities of the Church, nay shall defend the same and shall preserve them unimpaired and cause them to be kept in their integrity by their subjects. To none at all therefore of mankind be it lawful to infringe this page of our grant and will, or with rash presumption go against it. And if any one presume to attempt this let him know that he will incur the wrath of Almighty God and of the blessed Peter and Paul his Apostles. Given at Avignon on the Ides of June, of our pontificate the thirteenth year.

Nat. MSS Scot., ii, No. xxx

[The original bull is in the National Library of Scotland. From another bull, dated 9 Nov. 1330, in the Register House, it appears that Robert Bruce had undertaken to pay the pope 12,000 gold florins, equivalent to about £2,000, and that this sum was paid by David II. The payment of the sum can also be traced in the *Exchequer Rolls*.]

EDWARD BALLIOL'S CESSION OF THE SOUTHERN COUNTIES, 1334

In 1332 Edward Balliol (son of John Balliol), with a number of those who had been forfeited by Bruce, and with scarcely-disguised help from Edward III, had defeated the regent (Donald, Earl of Mar, acting for David II then eight years old) at Dupplin and had been crowned by his supporters, at Scone, as King of Scots. In 1333 the Scots were again heavily defeated, this time by an English army at Halidon Hill; and in May 1334 David II and

---

[1] This is the earliest indication of part of the content of the coronation oath.

his young queen were sent for safety to France. Meantime, in a
' parliament ' at Edinburgh, on 12 February 1334, Edward Balliol
had acknowledged Edward III as Lord Paramount of Scotland
and, in part return for the help he had received from England, had
surrendered the castle, town and county of Berwick to be forever
annexed to the kingdom of England. And now, by the following
charter of 12 June 1334, Edward Balliol supplemented the gift
of Berwick by handing over to England the whole of the southern
counties of Scotland.

Into these southern counties and castles Edward III promptly
sent English officials and English garrisons ; and the whole of
these southern lands had to be fought for to be re-won. Roxburgh
Castle was not finally regained from the English until 1460 (in a
siege which cost the life of James II) ; Berwick Castle was regained
in 1461—only to be lost again, for ever, in 1482.

Edward, by the grace of God king of Scots. . . . Know
ye that we (considering the purity of the love and goodwill
which we know our most excellent prince, dearest lord and
cousin, the lord Edward, illustrious king of England, has
had towards our person, and the great assistance in the
recovery of our heritage which he has lately given to us
from himself and his people, not without great and countless
expenses and perilous travails ; and desirous, in consideration of the foregoing, to prosper the said king of England
according to our opportunity at the time) have lately
willed and granted . . . to the foresaid king of England
2000 librates of land yearly, in competent places, on the
march of our kingdom of Scotland, adjacent to the kingdom
of England and pleasing to the foresaid king of England ;
and, in part of the value of the said 2000 librates of land,
have given . . . the castle, town and county of Berwick on
Tweed, and have promised that we shall cause the balance
of the said 2000 librates to be assigned and delivered to the
foresaid king of England in other competent places, as said
is, to be held by the same king of England and his heirs
with the knights' fees, patronage of churches and other
pertinents whatsoever, separated from the royal dignity
and crown of Scotland forever and annexed to the royal

dignity, crown and kingdom of England in all times to
come ; [*and have ratified the same, on 12 February last, in a
parliament at Edinburgh, with consent of the prelates, earls, barons,
knights and others of our kingdom.*]

We, therefore, wishing to fulfil our foresaid grant and
promise, being so made and accepted with the said assent
in the same parliament, as aforesaid, give, grant, render,
assign and by this our charter confirm . . . to the foresaid
king of England, the town, castle and county of Roxburgh,
the town, castle and forest of Jedburgh, the town and
county of Selkirk and the forests of Selkirk and Ettrick, the
town, castle and county of Edinburgh, with the constabu-
laries of Haddington and Linlithgow, the town, castle and
county of Peebles and the town, castle and county of
Dumfries . . . to be held and had by the same lord king
of England . . . with the knights' fees, patronage of
churches, chapels, religious houses and hospitals, and with
wards and other profits whatsoever which could pertain to
us, our heirs and successors, by reason of the vacancies of
the bishoprics of the kingdom of Scotland, of the lands,
tenements, goods and chattels, within the counties and
places foresaid pertaining to the same bishoprics, and with
hundreds, markets, fairs, forests, chases, parks, woods,
warrens and fishings, and with manors, demesnes, escheats,
forfeitures and reversions whatsoever, regalities, royal
liberties, free customs, ports as well of the sea as of fresh
waters, and with all the customs and maletotes, as well in
the town and port of the said town of Berwick as in the
other places and ports forenamed . . . separated from the
royal dignity and crown of Scotland forever, and annexed,
united and incorporated to the royal dignity, crown and
kingdom of England in all times to come, along with the
castle, town and county of Berwick aforesaid, in full satisfaction of the 2000 librates of land foresaid. . . .

Given by our hand, at Newcastle on Tyne, 12 June in
the 2nd year of our reign.

Foedera, ii, 888

THE TREATY OF BERWICK, 1357

David II, in fulfilment of the alliance with France, and also anxious himself to conduct a war against ' the enemy of England,' had invaded Northumberland and Durham in 1346, only to be defeated and taken prisoner at Neville's Cross.

After a captivity of eleven years he was released in accordance with the terms of the Treaty of Berwick. The enormous ransom imposed in that treaty was beyond Scotland's capacity. The first three instalments were paid in full, but thereafter the instalments fell heavily into arrears and various re-adjustments of the payments were later made. The full total was never paid. But the necessity of finding the ransom money led to a number of important constitutional developments (see *infra*, pp. 173 ff.) ; the payments made seriously affected Scotland's economy for more than a century.

This indenture made at Berwick on Tweed the third day of October the year of grace 1357 [1] between [seven commissioners named] on the part of the noble prince Edward king of England on the one part and [six commissioners named] on the part of Robert Stewart, guardian of Scotland, the prelates, lords and commons of Scotland on the other part, bears witness that it has been treated and agreed between the said parties that the noble prince our lord Sir David, king of Scotland, shall be freely delivered from prison and ransomed for a certain sum of money and under the conditions and in the manner as follows :

That is to say for one hundred thousand merks sterling to be paid during the ten years following the making of this agreement by these instalments, that is to say the ten thousand merks of the first payment on the Feast of the Nativity of St John the Baptist next to come [24 June], and other ten thousand merks on the Feast of the Nativity of St John the Baptist thereafter next following, and so from year to year ten thousand merks on the same Feast of the

[1] Ratified at Scone, 6 November 1357

Nativity of St John until the said sum of one hundred thousand merks shall have been paid in full.

And it is agreed that the payments shall be made . . . at Berwick on Tweed if it be in the hands of the king of England, and, if not, at Norham ; or, if it should please the king of England that the payments be made at Bamborough, then they shall be made there, and in that case the king of England shall give [safe] conduct from the march of England to those from Scotland who come to make the said payment. . . . And in case the Scots wish to make any of the payments at London, they shall be accepted there ; And the payments shall be made in sterling or in other coin of the king of England or in other coin of gold or silver of equal value to the coin of England.

Item that a truce shall be confirmed and observed by sufficient surety of letters and oaths between the king of England and all his good people in England and in Scotland, and also the Isle of Man, and the king of Scotland and all other people of Scotland and their adherents, by land and by sea, in all parts and places, without fraud or guile, until the said sum shall have been fully paid. And that Edward Balliol and John of the Isles and all other allies and adherents of the king of England shall be included in the said truce.

[Clauses for peaceful intercommunication and relations between England and Scotland during the truce, and for hostages (20 sons of the nobility, and 3 important nobles, in turns) until the ransom has been fully paid.]

Item, it is agreed that in case of default of payment at any of the said terms, the said king of Scotland, without any request or delay, shall come to England and render himself a prisoner of the king of England in the castle of Newcastle on Tyne within the three weeks next following the said term at which payment is in default, to remain a prisoner until payment of the arrears shall have been made, the hostages and the senior hostages also still remaining [in England] under the arrangements outlined above.

147

[Clauses adding that if the king is not able to come to render himself prisoner upon failure of the payments, he is to send in his place the Stewart, the Earl of Douglas and Thomas Moray (Lord Bothwell). And when the arrears have been paid in full, the king, or the special hostages, shall be allowed to return, but all the other hostages shall remain. If any hostage dies, another sufficient hostage to be sent in his place.

Very detailed arrangements binding the different estates in Scotland to fulfil their payments towards the ransom ; no papal bull of privilege to be sought, or to be valid, rendering all these arrangements, and the payments, null and void.]

And it is also agreed that the aforesaid king of England and prince on their part and the said king of Scotland on his part shall ratify, confirm and approve the aforesaid indenture, and everything contained therein, by letters patent under the great seals ; and they shall send the said letters, sealed, on the one part and on the other part, to the Warden of Berwick on Tweed on the Feast of St Martin next to come [11 November], or within the eight days next following at the latest, in order that they may be handed over one to the other. . . .

A.P.S., i, 518–21 (from the original)

DAVID II AND EDWARD III, 1363–4

The heavy taxation and other financial measures which were necessary to try to meet the instalments of David II's ransom pressed heavily upon the people in all ranks of life ; and in 1363 the Earl of Douglas, with Robert the Steward and the Earl of March, had risen in revolt against a king who had been ransomed at great cost but who used for the gratification of his own pleasures the sums which were raised for the payment of his ransom. The revolt was crushed ; but David II, not man enough to bear with his people the burden that the Treaty of Berwick had imposed upon Scotland, and always jealous of Robert the Steward as his immediate successor (*supra*, pp. 127 ff.), having proceeded to London in the autumn of 1363 there entered into the following agreement with Edward III. When, however, this agreement was brought by David before a Parliament at Scone in March 1364, parliament's refusal to ratify an arrangement which would have yielded all that Scotland had fought for since 1296 was voiced in terms that could not have been more forthright. We do not know the exact terms of the proposals put to the parliament by the king ; but, although we have no official record of the parliament of 1364, the ' Black Book ' gives us the terms of their complete rejection.

It is to be noted, however, that this was not the first occasion when David II proved himself to be an unworthy son of Robert Bruce, and that the proposals of 1363–4 were by no means new. In 1350, during his captivity, David had supplicated the Pope (Clement VI) for assistance and counsel. In his supplication he had pled that having been captive with some of his barons and knights for nearly four years, having no means of paying their ransoms, and being deprived by the fortune of war of the help of the king of France, there was nothing left but to implore divine help. But ' that the king of England may let the king of Scots and his fellow captives go free, he and his men would do homage to the king of England and his successors, and would assist him and them in their wars against France. The king of Scots would be cited to the parliaments and councils of the king of England. . . . Also, if the king of Scotland die without a lawful heir, the king of England or his son would be king of Scots. And the king of England and his people would have all the castles and fortresses of Scotland in their power until these promises are fulfilled ' (*Calendar of Papal Petitions*, i, 203). The endorsement to the petition was, ' Let letters be written to the king of France in accordance herewith ' ; and it is not difficult to imagine what the answer of the king of France would be.

With regard to the proposals of 1363–4, it should also be noted that a second indenture has survived, made at the same time, and possibly an alternative scheme. In this other indenture, all the Scottish castles, towns and fortresses occupied by England but which had previously been held by Robert Bruce were to be restored ; the Scots were to assist England in the Flemish wars ; the ' Disinherited ' and others were to be reinstated in their lands in Scotland ; there was to be a six hundred years' peace between England and Scotland ; and David was to be succeeded on the

Scottish throne *by one of the sons of Edward III who is not heir apparent to the Crown of England.* (*A.P.S.,* i, 494–5, from the original)

Abstract of Indenture, 27 November 1363

In an indenture at Westminster, in the presence of Edward III and David II, it was suggested [1] between the Privy Councils of England and Scotland [2] as a tentative scheme that :

[*Here follow the more important clauses*]

The king of Scotland should sound the estates of his realm as to whether they would agree that, if the said king of Scotland should die without an heir,[3] the king of England and his heirs kings of England shall succeed to the kingdom of Scotland. If that is agreed to, then,

The king of England shall yield up the town, castle and land of Berwick, as well as the castles of Roxburgh, Jedburgh and Lochmaben with their respective lands, and all other lands held by England which, at the time of his decease, were held by King Robert [Bruce [4]].

The outstanding arrears of the ransom shall be discharged, all future obligations cancelled, and the hostages released.

The name and title of the realm of Scotland shall be preserved with due honour, and separate ; there shall be no union or annexation with the realm of England ; and the king shall be styled, ' King of England and of Scotland.'

The king at his coronation (and, after having been crowned king of England, the king shall come to Scotland to be crowned there as king of Scotland, at Scone, on the royal chair which is to be restored to Scotland), shall

---

[1] The phraseology is very guarded ; it was only a suggestion put forward to try to secure peace and concord between the two realms.

[2] Only a few members of his council would be present with David II in London.

[3] The words *heir male* occur in the last clause of the document.

[4] See Edward Balliol's cession of the southern lands of Scotland, *supra,* p. 143.

swear to maintain the freedom of the church of Scotland so that it shall be subject only to the Holy See ; to maintain the laws, statutes and customs of the kingdom of Scotland as established under its former kings ; that he will not summon or constrain the people of Scotland to compear in England ; and that no benefice shall be conferred on any save Scotsmen.

He shall also swear that all officers of state, sheriffs, provosts, bailies, constables and other officers shall be Scotsmen ; that he will hold and maintain the prelates, earls, barons and all freeholders in their franchises, lands, rents and possessions ; and that he will impose no new prises, tallages, or exactions upon the realm of Scotland.

The king of Scotland shall sound the inclinations of his people in these matters and shall inform the king of England and his council thereof within fifteen days after Easter next to come [7 April 1364].

Foedera, iii, 715–16 ; A.P.S., i, 493–4 (from the original)

David II did sound the inclinations of his people in a parliament held at Scone on 4 March 1364, and received parliament's reply—

In the parliament held at Scone, 4 March 1363 [1364] . . . there having assembled and compeared the prelates and nobles of the kingdom who ought to be and could conveniently be there present, certain points were explained and read . . . which had been touched upon and spoken about between the council of the king of England and those who had lately been with our lord the king in London, whereby, if those points were conceded, peace could thereupon be obtained and confirmed.

And it was there expressly replied by the three estates that they were in no manner willing to concede, nor in any wise willing to assent to those points which had been sought by the king of England and his council as is above noted. . . .

A.P.S., i, 492–3 (from the ' Black Book ')

Chapter Ten

THE STEWARTS

The Accession of the Stewart Dynasty

On the death of David II (22 February 1370/71) Robert, the Steward, succeeded to the throne of Scotland as Robert II in virtue of the Act of Settlement of 1318 (*supra*, p. 130). But there was some dubiety about the legitimacy of Robert II's children by his first wife, Elizabeth Mure. We now know that he was granted a papal dispensation in 1347 for his marriage to Elizabeth Mure (they were within the fourth degree of consanguinity), but his son John, Earl of Carrick (later Robert III) was born some ten years before the dispensation was granted. By canon law the subsequent marriage of parents (when there was no impediment to the marriage) made their children legitimate; but there was some doubt whether a later dispensation could make legitimate a child born of parents who were within the forbidden degrees and who, at the time of his birth, had enjoyed no such dispensation. Was not such a child, if the parents were not ignorant of their relationship, born in incest? And could a papal dispensation, granted ten years after his birth, make John, Earl of Carrick, legitimate? Could he legitimately succeed his father on the throne? (See, in general, John Riddell, *Tracts, Legal and Historical*, 155 ff.; *Exchequer Rolls*, iv, cliii ff.).

There could be no question of the legitimacy of Robert II, or of his right of accession; but, with his accession, it was vital to secure and define the succession, for Robert II was already nearly 55 years old. Accordingly, (i) At Scone, in 1371, and immediately following the coronation of Robert II, John, Earl of Carrick, the eldest son of Robert II by his first wife, Elizabeth Mure, was declared to be the true successor and true heir to the crown—a declaration made with the unanimous consent of all the prelates, earls, nobles and the rest of the community there assembled. [And thereby it would appear that the canon law doctrine of legitimation *per subsequens matrimonium* became part of the civil law of Scotland : a doctrine that had been rejected in England at the council of Merton in 1236.]

(ii) In 1373, in a parliament at Scone, the order of succession to the throne was defined, *nominatim*, in the male line : firstly to John, Earl of Carrick and his heirs male ; then to Robert, Earl of Fife, and his heirs male ; then to Alexander of Badenoch, and his heirs male—these being the three surviving sons of Elizabeth Mure ; whom, and their heirs male all failing, then to David, Earl of Strathearn, and his heirs male ; then to Walter, Earl of Atholl, and his heirs male—these being Robert II's two sons by his second marriage to Euphemia Ross.

This question of the legitimacy of Robert III and his line, and the settlement of 1373 (under which there were some who felt that the sons whose legitimacy was dubious had been preferred to the sons whose status was unquestionable), is reflected in James I's actions against the houses of Strathearn and Atholl ; it is in the background of the assassination of James I ; and its echoes were heard as late as 1632, when the Earl of Menteith claimed the earldom of Strathearn with, it was said, a right to the crown then worn by Charles I (see *Scots Peerage*, i, 133–5).

1371.

On 26 March 1371, at Scone, Robert the Steward of Scotland, earl of Strathearn, nephew of lord David Bruce, illustrious king of Scotland, of renowned memory, lately deceased, was crowned and anointed king by the reverend father in Christ lord William de Laundelys, bishop of St Andrews.

A.P.S., i, 545 (from the ' Black Book ')

[On 27 March 1371] the most serene prince lord Robert, by the grace of God illustrious king of Scots, at Scone, at the time of his coronation (where there were present with him the prelates, earls, barons and the rest of the clergy and people of his kingdom), after the solemn rites of his anointing and coronation had been performed, and after a declaration had been made of the law by which the same most serene prince succeeded, and ought to have succeeded, to the lord David, king of Scotland, his uncle and prede-

THE EARLY STEWARTS

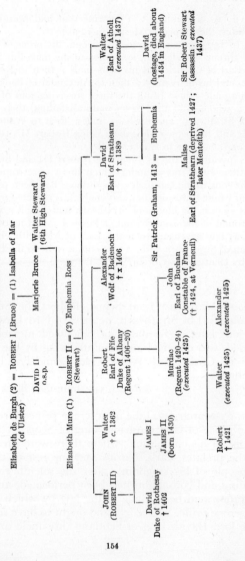

cessor, as well by nearness of blood as in accordance with the declaration of certain instruments [1] made in the time of lord Robert, king of Scotland, of illustrious memory, grandfather and predecessor of our same lord the king, there shown and read, also after he had received the wonted oaths of homage and fealty from the selfsame prelates, earls, barons and others of the clergy and people there being present, which oaths were of old used and wont to be given at the coronation of the kings of Scotland.

He wishing, after the manner and example of that same good king Robert, of renowned memory, his grandfather, to declare there, in presence of the clergy and people, his successor and true heir, although with regard thereto it was and is evident, yet, for the greater certainty, and with the unanimous consent and assent of the said prelates, earls, nobles and great men, he indicated, asserted and acknowledged, declared and willed that when he, by the divine dispensation, should happen to depart this life the lord John, earl of Carrick and Steward of Scotland, his first-born son, shall and ought to be his true and lawful heir and, the Lord so ordaining, shall and ought to succeed him, after his death, in the kingdom of Scotland, and, after him, shall and ought to sit upon the throne of his kingdom.

Which declaration so made by our said lord the king regarding his aforesaid eldest son and heir, for more certainty, as above, each of the prelates, earls, nobles, great men and others there present with his own voice, severally, for himself, his heirs and successors, asserted, affirmed, declared, acknowledged and willed that the selfsame lord John, surviving and living after the death of his aforesaid father, shall with the help of the divine grace, be king of Scotland as the lawful heir of his father, each promising in good faith, and with his hand upholden in token of faith-giving, that he will hold him for king and the lawful heir of his father, and will assist and defend him against all men whomsoever, and will also affix his seal to the writ or

---

[1] That is, the Act of Settlement of 1318 (see *supra*, p. 130)

instrument to be made hereupon, in token of his consent and promise aforesaid, when he shall be so required.

A.P.S., i, 546 (from the original instrument)

1373.

[On 4 April 1373] King Robert, holding his parliament at Scone, and wishing and desiring to avoid to the best of his ability the uncertainty of the succession and the evils and misfortunes which, in most kingdoms and places, happen, and in times past have happened from the succession of female heirs, and to avoid these for himself and his people, especially in times to come,

Of deliberate counsel, and with the consent and assent of the prelates, earls, barons and the rest of the chief men and nobles and of all others of the three estates or communities of the whole realm there assembled,

Declared, ordained and enacted that the sons of the king, of his first and second wives, now born, and their heirs male only, shall succeed one after another, in turn, to the said king in his kingdom and in the right of reigning in the manner and under the form and conditions underwritten, namely,

That the lord John, earl of Carrick and Steward of Scotland, the first-born son of the king himself, for the right of whose succession a declaration had been fully made in the immediately preceding parliament,[1] and his heirs male only, shall, after his death, succeed him in the kingdom and in the right of reigning ; and if the said lord John and his heirs male happen to fail (which God forbid) the lord Robert, earl of Fife and Menteith, the second-born son of our lord the king by his first wife, and his heirs male only, shall in turn and immediately succeed to the kingdom and the right of reigning ; and if the said lord Robert and such heirs of his happen also to fail (which God forbid) the lord Alexander, lord of Badenoch, the third-born son of our lord the king by the same wife, and his

[1] See *supra*, p. 153

heirs male only, shall, after their death, in like manner, in turn and immediately, succeed to the kingdom and the right of reigning ; and the said lord Alexander and his aforesaid heirs happening in like manner to fail (which God forbid), the said parties thus failing wholly, the lord David, earl of Strathearn, son of our lord the king born of his second wife, and his heirs male only, shall, in like manner, in turn and immediately, succeed to the kingdom and the right of reigning ; and the said lord David and his heirs aforesaid happening in like manner to fail, Walter, son of our lord the king, brother-german to the said lord David, and his heirs male only, shall in like manner succeed to the kingdom and the right of reigning ; and the aforesaid five brothers and their heirs male descending from them happening finally and wholly to fail (which God forbid), the true and lawful heirs of the royal blood and kin shall thenceforward succeed to the kingdom and the right of reigning.

A.P.S., i, 549 (from the original deed)

THE TREATY OF LONDON, 4 DECEMBER 1423

James I, succeeding his father, Robert III, as king of Scotland on 4 April 1406, had been captured by English pirates on 22 March 1406 and remained a prisoner in England until he was released in accordance with the Treaty of London (December 1423), returning to his own kingdom early in April 1424.

It is to be noted that :

(i) Ten thousand merks of the ransom were subsequently remitted as the dowry of Joan Beaufort, whom James married in February 1424 ; but

(ii) only 9,500 merks of the first instalment were paid, and only about 1,300 merks of the second instalment. The rest of the ransom was never paid.

(iii) The absence of many of the nobility as hostages in England helped James considerably in his efforts to consolidate the authority of the crown. Furthermore, of the descendants of Robert II and Euphemia Ross, Malise Graham of Strathearn (later Menteith) was a hostage in England from 1427 to 1453, and David Stewart of Atholl, sent as a hostage in 1424, died as a hostage, probably in 1434.

The main clauses of the Treaty of London are :

Inprimis that the said lord James, king of Scots, or his heirs or successors kings of Scots, shall well and faithfully pay to the aforesaid lord Henry, king of England and France, or his heirs or successors, or their deputes, in the Church of St Paul, London, in England, for the maintenance and expenses of the lord king James during the time of his stay in the kingdom of England, and elsewhere in the company of the kings of England, and from the time of his stay in England to the day on which he shall have returned to the kingdom of Scotland, or on which he shall be deemed to have returned, fory thousand pounds of good and legal money of England, to wit, In the aforesaid Church of St Paul, ten thousand merks of the aforesaid money within six months reckoned from the first day of his return to the kingdom [of Scotland], or from the first day on which he shall be deemed to have returned ; and each year thereafter following, the year beginning from the end of the year reckoned after the first day of his return aforesaid, or from the day on which he is deemed to have returned, as aforesaid, within six months from the beginning of each year so reckoned, ten thousand merks in the Church of St Paul aforesaid, until the said forty thousand pounds shall have been fully and wholly paid.

Item, that the said lord James, king of Scots, shall come (God willing) to the city of Durham or to the castle of Brancepeth, within eight days after the Feast of the Purification of the Blessed Virgin Mary [2 February] next to come, so that during the remainder of the month of February he may be able to make arrangements and to issue the necessary order with regard to his hostages and those who are willing and ought to remain as hostages for him and his deliverance. Item, that on the first day of the month of March next to come, the commissioners of the aforesaid Henry, king of England and France, deputed thereto, and the aforesaid James king of Scots and the ambassadors for and on behalf of the aforesaid kingdom of Scotland, or others to be appointed in their place, shall meet in the church of Durham, namely in order that the said King James and the commissioners of the aforesaid kingdom of Scotland may hand over and deliver to the commissioners of the aforesaid king of England and France, on the same first day, or at least before the last day of the same month of March, the persons who are to be handed over and delivered as hostages [1] for the deliverance of the said king James, and as security for the due observance of the appointment. Item that the said king James or the commissioners of the kingdom of Scotland aforesaid, shall truly and in fact hand over and deliver to the aforesaid commissioners and deputes of the aforesaid king of England and France, or of his heirs and successors, kings of England, before the aforesaid last day of March, in the city of Durham, for security for the payment of the said forty thousand pounds and the keeping of this appointment, the persons of the hostages whose names are contained in the schedule annexed hereto or other hostages of like value in property and rents acceptable to the aforesaid commissioners of the aforesaid king of England or his heirs and successors ; and in handing over the hostages the ambassadors and commissioners of the kingdom of Scotland aforesaid shall swear, each singly on the holy evangels, that the persons thus to be handed over as hostages are indeed the persons agreed upon as hostages and not others impersonating them.

Item, that within the same month of March the aforesaid king James or the ambassadors or commissioners of the aforesaid kingdom of Scotland shall deliver and hand over to the commissioners of the said Henry, king of England and France, or his heirs and successors, four letters obligatory [for the payment of the whole of the ransom] of the

[1] For the original hostages, and changes in the hostages, see E. W. M. Balfour-Melville, *James I, King of Scots*, App. D.

four underwritten burghs or towns of the kingdom of Scotland, sealed with their common seals, according to the form laid down in the schedule annexed hereto, saving always any change in the names of the same towns or burghs and of their provosts, bailies, or rectors, namely

One [letter obligatory] of the burgh of Edinburgh.

One of the burgh of Perth, commonly called St Johnston.

One of the burgh of Dundee.

One of the burgh of Aberdeen.

Rotuli Scotiae, ii, 241

CHAPTER ELEVEN

LAW AND ORDER

There are indications that after Bruce had secured Scottish independence in 1314 it still remained for him to consolidate the nation under his sovereignty. Barons who held estates in both England and Scotland were loth to give undivided allegiance which would involve the loss of their lands in one country or the other ; nobles of royal descent may have envied Bruce his crown ; and the pope's experiment in peace-making in 1317, which suggested that there was little prospect of a permanent settlement on the basis of Bruce's kingship, may have incited discord. These facts are the background of the first of the two acts printed below. The act should be read, too, in relation to the events of 1320— the conspiracy of William de Soulis, who possibly aimed at sup-planting Bruce, the severe punishment of his supporters by the 'Black Parliament,' and the demonstration of national unity contained in the letter of the barons to the pope.[1]

The second act which is printed shows the determination of Bruce's government to secure adequate defence against external foes ; it is the precursor of many similar acts passed in succeeding reigns.

Both acts are contained in the transcript of the statutes of the parliament of 1318 entered in the Register of the Abbey of Arbroath ; and since Bernard de Linton was at that time both Abbot of Arbroath and Bruce's chancellor there is no reason to doubt their accuracy.

ACTS OF 1318

Alsua the kyng hes statut and defendyt that nane be conspiratour na fyndar of taylis or of tithingis [2] thruch the quhilkis mater of discord may spryng betuix the kyng and his pepill. And gif ony sic be fundyn and attayntyt als sone

---

[1] *Supra*, p. 131   [2] *Narracionum seu rumorum* in the Latin version

he salbe takyn and be send to the kyngis prisoun and thar he sal be sikkerly kepyt quhil our lord the kyng haf said of him his will.

A.P.S., i, 472

Alsua it is ordanyt and assentyt that indurand the tym of were evir ilk lawyt man of the kynrik that hes x lib. in gudis sal haf for his body in the defence of the kynrik a gud suffyciand acton [1] a basnet [2] and gluffis of playt with a sper and a suerd and he that hes nocht an acton and a basnet sal haf a haberion [3] for his body and a hat of irn and gluffis of playt sa that ilkane sal be purveyit of the harnes forsayd at the octavis of pasch nixt for to cum. And quhasa evir he be that hes x lib. in gudis and hes nocht thir forsayd helpis he sal tyn al his gudis the ta half to the kyngis oise and the tothir half to the lord on quhais land he duellis. And the kyng wil that evir ilk schiref of the kynrik wyth the lordis of the placis inquer apon thir thyngis and thai sal mak wapynschawyn alson eftir the octavis of pasch forsayd. Alsua the kyng willis that ilk man hafand in gudis the valour of a kow sal haf a gud sper or a gud bow wyth a schaff of arowys that is to say xxiiii arowys undir the payn forsayd.

A.P.S. i, 473-4

ACTS OF 1357

The problems of government from 1357 until the end of David II's reign arose primarily from the burden of his ransom. If Scotland was to be able to pay the ransom, efforts had to be made to ensure prosperity by protecting and encouraging trade and by providing conditions of law and order in which economic life would be secure. The problem seems to have been complicated by David's own expensive tastes and lavish spending and possibly by a readiness on his part and on that of some of the magnates to interfere arbitrarily with the normal course of law.

[1] A leather jerkin, probably plated
[2] A steel headpiece or helmet   [3] A jacket of mail

The acts of 1357 which follow arose from those conditions : justice must not be hindered by the inefficiency of the judges and the ministers of the king ; the king must conserve the crown property, so that he can live of his own [1] ; the desirability of stable conditions is emphasised, with special reference to burghs and merchants. (See also David II's general charter to the burghs—*infra*, p. 215.)

Some of these acts represented pious aspirations rather than achievements ; for much the same sort of thing had to be said again in 1366 (*A.P.S.*, i, 498–9).[2]

Again there is no official record, and these acts are taken from the transcripts preserved in the ' Black Book.'

Item, that [the king] ordain that there be good and sufficient sheriffs and coroners who know and are able to exercise their offices and to give justice to every man, as is fitting ; and who also have good and sufficient bailies and officers for whom they must answer. And if any have been infeft in these offices of old, and shall be unable in their persons to exercise office, then in that case they shall present to the lord king other good and sufficient deputes to exercise office in their stead and for whom they must answer.

Item, it is ordained that the said lord our king, for his lifetime, shall call back into his hands all lands, rents and possessions, and customs, given and granted by him to any persons of any estate whatsoever ; and that all lands, rents and possessions which of old were wont to pertain to the demesne and royal crown shall remain in the hands of the king wholly and for ever without any alienation whatever, and he shall live on them ; so that the community of the kingdom, already burdened with the payment of the king's ransom, may not be further burdened with his expenses. And that the lord king renew the oath which he once took at his coronation, namely, that he will not alienate his demesne lands, possessions or rents pertaining

---

[1] The reference to the coronation oath, in which the king apparently swore not to alienate the crown lands, is the second indication of part of the content of that oath (see *supra*, p. 143, *note*).

[2] *Infra*, p. 180 ff.

to the crown ; and that, without mature counsel, revocations of lands and wardships or rents shall not be alienated.

Item, that firm peace shall be observed and kept everywhere throughout the realm between all subjects of our lord the king who are within his peace . . . so that no one henceforth make war against his neighbours under the full pain of forfeiture. And that this be proclaimed publicly in the present council.

Item, that all burghs and burgesses shall freely enjoy all their rights, liberties and privileges which they were wont to have in time of peace. And that henceforth no one presume to oppress them unjustly, either within burgh or without, under the pain of breaking the king's protection.

Item, that all foreign merchants, from wheresoever they may come, be allowed to enter peacefully to buy and to sell, as was lawfully done before ; and that all good coinage of the king of England, of gold or silver, be accepted throughout the kingdom of Scotland at the true value at which it is current in England.

A.P.S., i, 492

LEGISLATION AGAINST ' MAINTENANCE '—AN ATTEMPT TO RESTRICT RETINUES

1366. [*In Parliament of July 1366 it was enacted*] that no prelate, earl or baron or anyone of any rank, cleric or lay, shall ride, to the destruction of the land, with a greater retinue in persons or horses than becomes his rank, and that no-one shall lead with him spearmen or archers riding through the land unless there is a reasonable cause about which they shall be held to make an oath to the king's ministers holding an inquiry on this matter, on pain of imprisonment.

A.P.S., i, 499 (from the ' Black Book ')

GOVERNMENT

In the reigns of Robert II and Robert III the problem was largely a personal one, arising from the weakness—whether through age, infirmity or folly—of each of those on whom the hereditary right to govern successively devolved. In 1384, John, earl of Carrick, as heir of the ageing Robert II, was commissioned to execute the law. But in 1388, because of the ' infirmity ' of John, earl of Carrick, the earl of Fife (later duke of Albany) was chosen to have the power of the king to do justice, maintain the laws, and defend the kingdom (*A.P.S.*, i, 556). And it was this ' infirm ' earl of Carrick who became king in 1390 as Robert III.

By 1398 the tale of disorder is pitiable. The estates frankly laid responsibility at the door of the king himself, and, in the hope of remedy, appointed the duke of Rothesay as lieutenant and pressed for annual parliaments. The terms of Rothesay's appointment give us a further glimpse of the contents of the coronation oath, while the reason given for annual parliaments— that the lieges ' be servit of the law '—indicates the still curial nature of the Scottish Parliament.

1384.   Item, because our lord the king, for certain causes, is not able himself to attend regularly and thoroughly in all things to the execution of the government and law of his kingdom, he has willed, granted and ordained, with the counsel and decision of his council, that his eldest son and heir the lord Earl of Carrick shall execute the common law, everywhere through the realm, to all persons suffering grievance or wrong from all and sundry persons contravening the law, either by himself or by those whom he may depute and for whom the earl will be held answerable to the king and council.

A.P.S., i, 550 (from the Haddington MSS)

1398.   In diebus illis non erat lex in Scocia sed quilibet potencior minorem oppressit et totum regnum fuit unum latrocinium. Homicidia depredaciones et incendia et cetera maleficia remanserunt inpunita et justicia utlegata extra regni terminos exulavit.

[In those days there was no law in Scotland, but he who was strong oppressed the weak and the whole kingdom was one den of thieves. Homicides, ravagings, and fire-raisings and all other evil deeds remained unpunished ; and justice, outlawed, was in exile outwith the bounds of the kingdom.]

'Chronicle' in *Register of Moray*, No. 303

1399.

The act of the consail generale haldyn at Perth the xxvii day of Januare the yhere of grace m ccc nynty and acht apon syndry poyntes touchande oure lorde the kyng and the estate of his reaulme giffyn to deliberacion of the thre commons of the kynryke thare gaderyt :

Quhare it is deliveryt that the mysgouvernance of the reaulme and the defaut of the kepyng of the common law sulde be imput to the kyng and his officeris : and tharfore gife it lykeis oure lorde the kyng til excuse his defautes he may at his lykyng gerre calle his officeris to the quhilkis he hes giffyn commission and accuse thaim in presence of his consail : and thair ansuere herde the consail sal be redy to juge thair defautes, syn na man aw to be condampnyt quhil he be callit and accusit.

Item sen it is wele sene and kennyt that oure lorde the kyng for seknes of his person may nocht travail to governe the realme na restreygne trespassours and rebellours it is sene to the consail maste expedient that the duc of Rothesay be the kyngis lieutenande generally throch al the kynrike for the terme of thre yhere, hafande ful powere and commission of the kyng to governe the lande in al thyng as the kyng sulde do in his person gife he warre present : that is to say to punys trespassours, till restreygne trespassis and to trete and remitte with the condicions efter folowande, that is to say that he be oblygit be his letteris and suorne til governe his person and the office til hym committit with the consail general and in the absence of thaim with the consail of wyse men and lele, of the quhilkis there arre the namys : in the firste the duc of Albany, the lorde of Brechyn, the byschopis of Andriston, Glasgu and Aberden, the erlys

of Douglas, of Ross, of Moref and Crauforde, the lorde of
Dalketh, Schir Thomas the Hay, constable, Schir Wilyhem
of Keth, marchal, Schir Thomas of Erskyne, Schir Patrik
the Graham, Schir John of Levynston, Schir Wilyhem
Stewart, Schir John of Remorgny, Adam Forstar, the
abbot of Halyrudehous, the archiden of Louthyan and
Maister Water Forstar ; the quhilkis consail general and
special sal be obligit be thair letteris and suorne til gife
hym lele consail for the common profite, nocht hafande ee
to fede na freyndschyp, ande in efter the said duc be
suorne til fulfyl efter his power all the thyngis that the
kyng in his crownyng wes suorne for til do to haly kyrke
and the pupyl syn in to thir thyngis he is to ber the kyngis
power, that is to say the fredume and the rycht of the
kirke to kepe undamyste the lawys and the lovable cus-
tumes to gerre be kepit to the pupil, manslaerys, reiferis,
brynneris and generaly all mysdoeris thruch strynthe til
restreygnhe and punyse and specialy cursit men, heretikis
and put fra the kyrke at the requeste of the kyrke to restreygne, and that the kyng be obliste that he sal nocht lette
his office na the execucion of it be na contremandmentis as
sumquhile has bene seyne and gife ocht be done in the
contrare be letteris or ony other maner thruch our lorde the
kyngis bydding that contremandment be of na valu na of
effect na the forsaid lieutenant be nocht haldyn tyl ansuere
suylke contremandmentis na be nocht essoynyhet thruch
vertu of thaim that he doys nocht his office.

A.P.S., i, 572–3 (from the Haddington MSS)

1399.   Item it is ordanyt that ilke yhere the kyng sal halde
a parlement swa that his subjectis be servit of the law the
qwhilk sal begyn on the morne efter all halow day for there
thre yhere to cum.

A.P.S., i, 573 (from the Haddington MSS)

DEATH OF THE DUKE OF ROTHESAY, 1402

When it proved necessary to restrain the duke of Rothesay in a career of vice and folly, the earls of Albany and Douglas, obtaining the king's consent to their taking some action, arrested Rothesay and imprisoned him at Falkland, where, according to Bower (?1440), he died ' of dysentery or, as others would have it, of starvation ' (*sive, ut alii volunt, fame*).[1] It is Hector Boece, as translated by Bellenden (? *c.* 1510) who states categorically that Albany ' inclusit ' Rothesay ' in ane toure but ony mete or drynk ' [2] and gives the picturesque details which Scott worked into *The Fair Maid of Perth*. Wyntoun (? *c.*1410), on the other hand, merely states that

> Our Lord the kingis eldest sone . . .
> Honest, habill and avenand . . .
> Cunnand in to litterature
> A seymly persone in stature . . .
> Yauld his saule til his creatoure.[3]

The official version was given in a council held on 16 May 1402, when Robert, duke of Albany, and Archibald, earl of Douglas, were absolved of all responsibility for the death of the duke of Rothesay, who ' in castro Sanctiandree primo custodiri deindeque apud Faucland in custodia deteneri ubi ab hac luce divina providencia et non aliter migrasse dinoscitur ' [4]—' he departed this life through the divine dispensation and not otherwise.'

BATTLE OF HARLAW, 1411

The conception of Harlaw as a struggle between Highlander and Lowlander for domination over Scotland is a later embroidery. The affair arose mainly from a dispute over the earldom of Ross, to which Donald of the Isles had a claim in right of his wife,

---

[1] *Scotichronicon*, xv, 12
[2] *Chronicles* (trans. Bellenden), Scot. Text. Soc. edn., ii, 361–2
[3] Wyntoun, ix, 23
[4] *A.P.S.*, i, 582 (from the ' Black Book ')

HARLAW (1411)

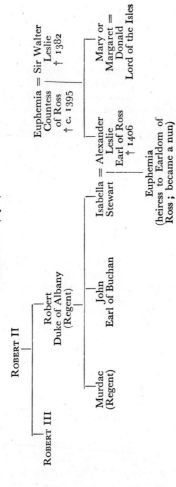

ROBERT II
—
ROBERT III   Robert
Duke of Albany
(Regent)

Murdac
(Regent)   John
Earl of Buchan

Euphemia = Sir Walter
Countess   Leslie
of Ross   † 1382
† c. 1395

Isabella = Alexander
Stewart   Leslie
Earl of Ross
† 1406

Mary or = Donald
Margaret   Lord of the Isles

Euphemia
(heiress to Earldom of
Ross ; became a nun)

but which Albany had contrived to have conferred on his own son, the earl of Buchan. The table on page 169 shows the relationship.

The opposing commanders at the battle were cousins, with an equal proportion of Highland blood, and Mar's army, although it included Aberdeen burgesses and other Lowlanders rallied by the sheriff of Angus, also included many Highlanders. Moreover, Mar himself was no model of civilisation, being an illegitimate son of the Wolf of Badenoch and a leader of caterans who had become earl of Mar only by compelling the widowed countess to marry him. Donald's advance towards Aberdeen was to recover the lands of the earldom of Ross in Banff, Aberdeen and Kincardine. (There is a full discussion of the whole question in *Trans. Gaelic Soc. of Inverness*, xxx, 267 ff.).

A retour of Andrew Tulidef as heir of William, his father, who had fallen at Harlaw, in a third of Ledyntusche and Rothmaes (held of the bishop of Aberdeen), related that Andrew, ' licet minoris etatis existit, tamen secundum quoddam statutum consilii generalis ex privilegio concesso heredibus occisorum in bello de Harelaw pro defensione patrie est hac vice legitime etatis ' (*Register of Aberdeen*, i, 215, 9 May 1413). From this it appears that there had been an act of council like that at Twizelhauch on 24 August 1513, before Flodden, whereby the heir of any man killed in the campaign was to have his ward, relief and marriage of the king free, ' dispensand with his aige quhat eild that evir he be of.' (*A.P.S.*, ii, 278 ; *Acts of the Lords of Council in Public Affairs*, 1).

The battle of Harlaw took place in Marr, on the vigil of St James the Apostle [24 July] in the year of the Lord 1411, because Donald of the Isles, with ten thousand islesmen and his men of Ross, made a warlike invasion, ravaging all the land and intending to sack the town of Aberdeen and subject the whole country as far as the Tay to his dominion. He was manfully resisted by Alexander Stewart, earl of Marr, with Sir Alexander Ogilvy, sheriff of Angus, . . . and with all the men he could raise from Mar, Garioch, Angus, Mearns and Buchan. . . . Donald himself was put to flight. . . . On the other side [Mar's] were slain . . .

the warlike Robert David[son], provost of Aberdeen, with many of his fellow burgesses.

Extracta e variis cronicis Scocie, 215

ACCOUNTS OF THE CUSTUMARS OF LINLITHGOW

The following extracts from the accounts of the custumars of Linlithgow for 1413–14 and 1418–20 illustrate the weakness of the government during the imprisonment of King James I, while the regency was held by Robert, duke of Albany, and his son Murdoch. It appears that a magnate like James Douglas, brother of the earl of Douglas, could raid the customs either by purloining them from the custumars or by extorting them directly from merchants ; and that he could evade paying customs on his own merchandise.

1413-14. *Eight pounds is allowed to Norman Young, one of the custumars making account,* ' in that James of Douglas, brother of the Earl, seized him in the town of Linlithgow and carried him to Abercorn and imprisoned him there until he had handed over to him the said eight pounds, on which matter the Lord Governor should be consulted.'

And the account closes with ' And thus there are unaccounted for £132 18s 4d which they [the custumars] say they have neither received nor delivered, but that the aforesaid James of Douglas seized and compelled various merchants, and by threats extorted from them, £78 12s 8d, as appeared by the letters of the said James, delivered in exchequer, which say that he has received that sum from various merchants from the custom of the said burgh, and the custumars will give the names of the merchants to the Lord Chamberlain. And Walter of Haliburton, husband of the Duchess [of Rothesay] seized from various merchants of the same town £54 5s 8d in a like manner, on which matter the Lord Governor should be consulted.'

E.R., iv, 193

1418-20. 'Thus there are unaccounted for £244 6s 2½d, of which sum those making the account swear that Walter of Haliburton, husband of the Duchess of Rothesay, seized from various merchants in the town of Linlithgow, and partly from the said custumars making account, whom to that end he took to [the Isle of] Fidra and imprisoned them there, saying that £235 8s 3d was due to him for the pension payable to his wife, the Duchess of Rothesay ; on which matter the Lord Governor should be consulted. Item, they say that James of Douglas, brother of the Earl, placed in ships at the port of Blackness, wool, skins and hides belonging to him, on which customs to the extent of £8 17s 11½d should have been paid, but of which he gave no satisfaction to the custumars, as appeared by his letters under his seal, relating to this, shown at the account ; on which matter the Lord Duke [of Albany] should be consulted.'

'Memorandum, the custumars of Linlithgow and the clerk of cocket there, questioned on oath whether they knew of any taking goods forth of the realm without payment of customs, said that James of Dundas of that ilk sent from Queensferry four serplates [1] of wool and one of skins and caused them to be entered in the ship of Henry fan Moustre. Item, the same James and Matthew Crukschank caused thirteen serplates of wool to be placed in the ship of Thomas of Armyddil without payment of customs. Item, there were sent from Abercorn thirteen serplates of wool and skins, on which no customs had been paid ; on all of which the Lord Governor should be consulted.'

E.R., iv, 320

[1] a *serplait* was eighty stones

CHAPTER TWELVE

PARLIAMENT

This period brought many important developments in the structure and organisation of the Estates of the Realm. The principal incentive was the government's financial difficulty in the period immediately after the English wars, reinforced by the burden of David II's ransom.

A distinction emerged between the full and formal meeting of the King's Council in Parliament summoned upon forty days' notice, and the less formal General Council which could be summoned at shorter notice and which lacked Parliament's judicial competence but was equally competent in political business, legislation and taxation.[1]

Financial pressure led to consultation with representatives of the burghs, first in 1326, outwith the parliamentary organisation, but gradually from 1357, as a result of the ransom negotiations, in General Council and finally in Parliament.

Simultaneously, there was an extension of parliamentary function, expressing itself most forcibly in 1366 in criticism and restriction of Crown authority.[2]

In 1367 another development appeared—the delegation of general parliamentary authority to a commission.[3] At first, like the contemporary committee of the Auditors of Causes and Complaints, and the committee for Falsed Dooms which evolved to relieve Parliament of certain judicial functions, this was an attempt to solve the practical difficulties involved in the meeting of a mediaeval Parliament. But a commission, unlike the committees, had the full power of Parliament and need not report back to Parliament. Its political possibilities, moreover, soon became apparent and were expressed in 1368 when it was declared *non expediens* for the whole community to discuss the state of the kingdom, the king and manner of his living.[4]

It must again be stressed that most of the excerpts from the

[1] *Infra*, p. 184   [2] *Infra*, p. 180 ; cf. *supra*, p. 166
[3] *Infra*, p. 185   [4] *Infra*, p. 185

Acts of the Parliaments of Scotland are taken from early transcripts or lawyers' collections, upon which we are dependent through the loss of the original rolls and registers.

BURGHS AND PARLIAMENT [1]

Representatives of the burghs were probably consulted on the making of the treaty with France in 1295–6 when the consent of the prelates, earls, barons and *communitates villarum* of Scotland was recorded and the seals of the burghs of Aberdeen, Perth, Stirling, Edinburgh, Roxburgh and Berwick were appended to the treaty in token of their assent. Their assent, however, does not necessarily imply their presence as one of the estates in Parliament or General Council. Again, in 1326, when burgesses along with earls, barons and free tenants promised Robert I the tenth penny, the indenture does not make any suggestion that the agreement was made *in* the Parliament of Cambuskenneth which was being held at the same time.[2]

The next mention of consultation of burgess representatives in national affairs comes when money was required in 1357 for David II's ransom. Three General Councils were held in that year. In the first, in January, there were separate meetings of all three estates but there is no definite evidence that burgesses were members of Council. In September, too, there is some doubt as to their membership, but in November the proceedings of the Council in detailed matters of burghal privileges and trade regulations show merchant participation. The record of these proceedings mentions the *Tres Communitates* but as it survives only in the *Blak Buik*, a transcript of a time when the ' three estates ' was the common description, that evidence cannot be relied upon alone. It is possible that burgh representatives had been finding a place in General Councils and in Parliaments between 1326 and 1357 but the evidence is too indefinite for any certain conclusion.[3]

After 1357 parliamentary record is still fragmentary, but in 1364 the *Three Estates* in *Parliament* are said to have rejected Edward III's succession proposals,[4] although Parliament is other-

---

[1] See R. S. Rait, *Parliaments of Scotland*, pp. 238 ff.
[2] *Infra*, p. 175 [3] cf. *Eng. Hist. Rev.*, lix, 79–87
[4] *Supra*, p. 151

wise said to have consisted of only prelates and barons, this perhaps suggesting outside consultation with the burgesses on an important matter with financial implications.

In 1366 there is no doubt about the inclusion of burgess representatives in Parliament—*qui ad hoc fuerunt ex causa summoniti*, stressing the financial purpose of their presence. This qualification in burgess summons continued as opposed to the *more debito et solito* of the other Estates, but after 1370 it gradually lapsed and burgess representation was regarded as normal.

1326.

Indenture whereby the earls, barons, burgesses and free tenants of Scotland granted a tenth penny to King Robert, 15 July 1326

The present indenture bears witness that, on the fifteenth day of the month of July, in the year from the incarnation of our Lord One thousand three hundred and twenty-sixth, the most serene Prince Lord Robert, by the grace of God the illustrious King of Scots, holding his full Parliament at Cambuskenneth, and the earls, barons, burgesses and all the other free tenants of his kingdom convening there, it was declared by the same Lord the King that the lands and rents, which used of old to belong to his Crown, had by divers donations and transfers, made on the occasion of war, been so diminished that he had not maintenance becoming his station without the intolerable burdening and grievance of his commons : Wherefore, he earnestly requested of them that, as he had sustained many hardships both in his person and in his goods for the recovery and protection of the liberty of them all, they would be pleased, from the gratitude that became them, to find a way and manner whereby he might be suitably maintained as became his station and with less grievous burden of his people, who, all and each, earls, barons, burgesses, and free tenants as well within liberties as without, holding of our Lord the King or of any other superior within the realm mediately or immediately, of what condition soever they were, considering and confessing that the foresaid reasons of our Lord the King were true, and how very many other advantages had in their times accrued to them through him, and that his request was reasonable and just, after a common and diligent discussion of the premises, unanimously, thankfully and cheerfully granted and gave to their Lord the King aforesaid annually, at the terms of Martinmas and Whitsunday proportionally, for the whole time of the life of the said King, the tenth penny of all their fermes and rents, as well of their demesne lands, and wards as of their other lands whatsoever within liberties and without, as well within burghs as without, according to the old extent of lands and rents in the time of our Lord of good memory Alexander, by the grace of God the illustrious King of Scots last deceased, to be faithfully made by his officers, the destruction of war alone excepted, in which case a deduction shall be made from the tenth penny above granted, according to the amount of the rent which for the reason foresaid can not be levied from the lands and rents foresaid, as shall be found by an inquest to be faithfully made by the sheriff of the place : provided that all such money shall be wholly applied to the use and profit of our said Lord the King, without any remission to be made to any one whatsoever ; and if he shall make a donation or remission from such money before it be conveyed into the King's treasury and fully paid, the present grant shall be null and of no force nor effect. And, whereas certain nobles of the realm claim such liberties that the King's servants may not be able to exercise their office within their lands, by which the payment to be made to our Lord the King may chance to be hindered, all and sundry claiming liberties of this sort did take in hand to our Lord the King to cause the portions effeiring to themselves and their tenants to be fully paid by their officers to the officers of the King at the appointed terms ; which if they do not, the King's sheriffs, each in his own sheriffdom, shall distrain the tenements of such liberties, by royal authority, for the making of such payment. On the other hand our Lord the King, weighing and considering with satisfaction the gratitude and goodwill of his people, has graciously granted to them that, from Martinmas next to come, namely, the first term of making payment, he shall not impose any collections nor take any prisage or carriages, unless when on a journey or in passing through the kingdom, after the manner of his predecessor King Alexander aforesaid, for which prisage and carriages full payment shall be made on the nail ; and that all large purveyances of the King, with their carriages, shall be made entirely without prisage ; and that the King's officers shall make payment in hand, without delay, for everything in making such large purveyances, according to the common market price of the country. Also it was consented and agreed between our Lord the King and the community of his kingdom that, upon the death of the said King, the grant of the tenth penny aforesaid shall immediately cease ; in such manner however that full satisfaction be made for the terms past before the death of our said Lord the King, and that neither by the premises or any of them, after the said grant has ceased, shall prejudice in any way be done to the heirs of our said Lord the King or the community of his kingdom, but that everything shall return to and remain in the same condition in which it was before the day of the present grant. In testimony of all which, to the one part of this indenture, remaining in the hands of the said earls, barons, burgesses and free tenants, is affixed the common seal of the realm, and to the other part, remaining in the hands of our Lord the King, the seals of the earls, barons and the other greater free tenants, along with the common seals of the burghs of the kingdom in name of themselves and of the whole community, are of common consent affixed. Given the day, year and place aforesaid.

Nat. MSS Scot., ii, No. xxvii. The Latin text of the original indenture is in *A.P.S.*, i, 475, and is taken from a transcript made on 27 February 1328 (*A.P.S.*, i, 483–4).

January 1357.

Representatives of the burghs first came to General Council when money was required for David II's ransom.

On 17 January 1357 Robert Stewart, lieutenant for king David, *de unanimi et expresso consensu et assensu omnium prelatorum procerum ac totius communitatis regni Scocie* appointed ambassadors to treat with the king of England about King David's release.

[*In witness to the letters patent* [1] *are appended*] the seals of the venerable fathers in Christ William, bishop of Glasgow, and John, bishop of Dunkeld, in the name and on behalf of all the clergy; and the seals of the noble men lord Patrick of Dunbar, Earl of March, Thomas Stewart, Earl of Angus, and William de Keith, marischal of Scotland, in the name and on behalf of all the nobles and barons; and the common seals of the burghs of Aberdeen, Dundee, Perth and Edinburgh in the name and on behalf of all the burgesses and the whole community.

Given in the full council of the king held at the town of St John at Perth [17 January 1357].

A.P.S., i, 515 (from the original)

September 1357

Know everyone by the present letters that we Alexander Gylyot, Adam Tore, and John Goldsmith of Edinburgh; John Mercer, John Gill and Robert de Gatmilk of Perth; Laurence de Garvok, William de Leith, and John Crab of Aberdeen; Master John de Somerville and Robert Kyd of Dundee; Roger Phipill and Thomas Johnson of Inverkeithing; Richard Hendchyld and Richard Scroger of Crail, Nicholas, rector of schools, and David Comyn of Cupar, Laurence Bell and Adam de Kirkintilloch of Saint Andrews, Richard de Cadzow and John Clerk of Montrose, John de Burgh and William Sauser of Stirling, John Johnson and William de Saltoun of Linlithgow, Adam de Haddington and Adam de Congleton of Haddington, Simon Potter and Peter Waghorn of Dumbarton, Patrick Clerk and Patrick Reid of Rutherglen, Andrew Adamson and Andrew de Ponfret of Lanark, William de Duncoll and Thomas

---

[1] i.e. appointing the ambassadors

Lang of Dumfries, Nicholas Johnson and John Williamson
of Peebles, aldermen, merchants and burgesses most eager
for the deliverance of our lord king David from the prison
of lord Edward, illustrious king of England, with the
consent and will of all the communities of the said burghs
and their adjacent parts, make, constitute and ordain by
our present letters, as true procurators, agents and special
ambassadors of all the burgesses and merchants of the said
realm of Scotland, Alexander Gylyot, Adam Tore, John
Goldsmith, John Mercer, John Gill, Robert de Gatmilk,
Laurence de Garvok, William de Leith, John Crab, Master
John de Somerville and Robert Kyd, burgesses of Edinburgh,
Perth, Aberdeen and Dundee, giving to them, and six or
four of them, full and free power and special mandate to
agree finally with the council of the aforesaid lord king of
England upon the liberation of our lord king David aforesaid and to agree to, affirm and approve in our name and
in the name of all burgesses and merchants of the whole
realm of Scotland, all and singular treaties and agreements
made, held or to be made between the said council of the
lord king of England and the prelates and other nobles of
the realm of Scotland and whatsoever points contained
within them which touch upon or can in any way touch
upon the liberation of our said lord king David ; and to
admit and acknowledge that we and all other burgesses
and merchants of the said realm of Scotland, our heirs and
successors, each one of us and them are held and obliged
as principals and as a whole to the said lord king of England,
his heirs and successors, on the redemption of our aforesaid
lord, king of Scotland, in the sum of 100,000 merks sterling
to be paid to the same lord king of England or his procurators in the places and at the times agreed or to be
agreed in the said treaties and agreements.

A.P.S., i, 517 (from the original deed)

November 1357.

The Council at Scone made many far-reaching provisions for
raising money to pay David II's ransom. The king was to be

allowed to buy all wool and woolfells in the kingdom at 4 merks a sack of wool and 4 merks for 200 woolfells, a census was to be taken of all rents, livestock and goods in the country, a new assessment was to be made of property so that it could be taxed *secundum verum valorem*, alienations of lands and possessions belonging to the Crown *ab antiquo* were to be revoked, the privileges of the burghs were reaffirmed, foreign merchants were to be allowed free entry for trade—and all this is recorded as

. . . concordatum est et assensum per tres communitates ibidem existentes.

A.P.S., i, 491 (from the 'Black Book')

July 1366.

In July 1366 we find burgh representatives in Parliament, summoned there *ad hoc ex causa*.

The Parliament held at Scone the twentieth day of July, the year of grace one thousand three hundred and sixty-six, and of the reign of our Lord King David the thirty-seventh : summoned and called, in manner due and wont, the Bishops, Abbots, Priors, Earls, Barons, free tenants, who hold of our Lord the King in chief, and from each burgh certain burgesses who were for a certain purpose and a special cause summoned thereto : compearing all those who ought, could, or would conveniently be present, certain others however being absent some of whom were lawfully excused, but others as of contumacy absented themselves, namely, William Earl of Ross, Hugh of Ross, John of the Isles, John of Lorn and John de Hay : Whereas the said Parliament was chiefly, among other things, appointed to deliberate, with the consent and assent of those above named, upon the treaty of peace to be made with the king and kingdom of England, in the form and regarding the points last brought back by the ambassadors ; and concerning full payment to be made of the ransom of our Lord the King, at the conclusion of the truce which is to last from this time for three years, in case that peace cannot in the meantime be renewed or farther truce be obtained ; and regarding the necessary expenses of the King and his ambassadors then about to be sent into England. First and chiefly, with respect to the matter of the peace, it had been ordained that the ambassadors who were lately in England should be sent to England therefor, namely, the Lord Bishop of St Andrews, Sir Robert of Erskyn, Master Walter of Wardlau and Gillebert Armistrang, as having already full commission to treat of peace, so that it may be established well and lasting between the kingdoms, conceding all things which, in the first instrument made under the seals of the Lords, were for the sake of peace conceded ; and farther, treating concerning a fourth point, namely, the aid of soldiers to be furnished by each party to the other, how it may best be done and with least burden, as in the last instrument made thereupon under the seals as above stated, they were charged upon that point. And farther, failing such treaty, to negotiate for an extension of the truce to the end of twenty-five years, paying the sum of ransom money which remains due ; namely, every year four thousand pounds as was contained formerly in the treaty. As to the second point, it was thus ordained, that, inasmuch as by the returns here made, both the old extents and the true values of all revenues of churches and lands, as well ecclesiastical as secular, are now surely ascertained, there should be taxed also all the goods of burgesses and of husbandmen, except, for the present, white sheep, and a return thereof made to the Council at Edinburgh against the feast of the nativity of the blessed Virgin next to come. And then, the total sum being ascertained of the true value of all the goods of the whole kingdom, a contribution shall be ordained to be generally levied, and pound shall be held equal to pound, so that immediately thereupon there may be raised eight thousand merks for the expenses of the King, and for payment of his debts within the kingdom, and for the expenses of the ambassadors, and no more, inasmuch as the great custom is appointed for the said payment of four thousand pounds, towards the ransom as aforesaid, until the ambassadors shall return. And from this follows plainly the ordinance as to the third point, namely, that whereas our Lord the King has for greater security assigned his great custom for the payment of the said four thousand pounds towards his ransom money yearly, the said four thousand pounds shall be raised from the said contribution to be levied, and two thousand merks also out of the said contribution, a thousand merks namely, to pay the King's debts and to meet his expenses in the meantime, and a thousand merks for the expenses of the ambassadors ; which two thousand merks have been advanced in loan so that they might be had immediately, namely, by the barons a thousand merks, by the clergy six hundred merks, by the burgesses four hundred merks, which shall be refunded to them when the said contribution has been levied, the sureties for payment to the burgesses being Sir Robert of Erskyn and Sir Walter of Byger, Chamberlain of Scotland.

And it was, in the said Parliament at the instance of the three estates, by the King expressly conceded and also publicly proclaimed, first, that to every one common justice be done without favour shown to any and without exception of person ; and that letters issuing from the King's chancery or otherwise, written by other officers having charge to do justice, for justice doing, shall not be recalled by whatsoever other letters under whatsoever seal ; but that it shall be lawful for the officers to whom such letters are addressed, notwithstanding of them, to do justice and to send them back endorsed.

Also, that since the estates have now burdened themselves with so heavy a payment, both for meeting the ransom of our Lord the King and for the necessaries and expenses of himself and of his ambassadors, none of the sums which are ordained for this purpose shall be applied to any other uses whatsoever, by gift, remission or otherwise, but solely to those purposes for which they are as aforesaid severally ordained.

Also, that churchmen and their lands bestowed in alms shall enjoy their liberties and privileges, and that no other burdens or imposts be laid upon them beyond the burdens conceded in Parliament. And if there be any who impede the assedation of teinds, that they shall be prevented by the King on the complaint of those who are aggrieved in this matter, so that they may enjoy their teinds peaceably and in their integrity, under pain of excommunication on the part of the clergy, and a fine of ten pounds to the King.

Also, that nothing shall be taken from the commons for the use of the King without prompt payment ; nor yet shall anything be taken in prisage except in place and manner as is used and ought to be done, [and] there shall be made, in due and accustomed time, prompt and due payment for the same.

Also, that those rebels, namely, of Atholl, Argyll, Badenoch, Lochaber and Ross and others, if any there be, in the northern parts or elsewhere, shall be arrested by the King and his power, to underlie common justice, and specially to pay the contribution, and otherwise be corrected as shall be most conducive to peace and the advantage of the community and the kingdom.

Also, that all the officers of the King, namely, sheriffs and other inferior officers, both within burgh and without, shall be obedient to the Chamberlain and other superior ministers, under pain of their removal from their offices, without hope of being afterwards restored to the same.

Also, that no one be sent with horses to quarter upon religious persons, parsons, vicars or husbandmen, nor shall any, with any horses whatsoever, be sent into the country to consume the goods, corn or meadows of husbandmen or others ; nor shall any one presume this to do under the penalty which ought to be inflicted for such offence, according to the extent of the offence and the quality of the person.

> *Nat. MSS Scot.*, ii, xlii ; *A.P.S.*, i, 498-9
> (from the ' Black Book ')

After Edward III's proposals to David II [1] had been rejected *per tres communitates* the estates made provision that the truce should be amended and the ransom paid.

1364.

The king, therefore, with the counsel and assent of the said estates forthwith ordered his ambassadors to be sent to England having full commission for this matter . . . and the aforenamed prelates and nobles agreeably undertook and promised each one singly in the faith and fealty by which he was bound to our lord king . . . that, immediately after the envoys had returned from England, when they were summoned or warned by royal letters under whatsoever seal (*sub quocunque sigillo*), they would personally convene at the place and time assigned to them in these letters and according to what was related by the messengers themselves would discuss the question of the king and the affairs of the realm with united counsel and unanimous consent as if they were lawfully summoned on forty days as to a parliament, and they would raise no exception or excuse as to the shortness of time [of summons] or otherwise.

> *A.P.S.*, i, 493 (from the ' Black Book ')

[1] *Supra*, p. 151

COMMISSIONS

1367.

[*In the year 1367 the three estates of the kingdom having met at Scone*] certain persons were elected by them [the three estates] to hold the parliament, and to the others licence was given to return home on account of the harvest.

A.P.S., i, 501 (from the ' Black Book ')

1369.

In the Parliament held at Perth on 6 March 1368/9 with continuation of the following days. . . .

. . . since the same parliament was ordained to be held on the five certain points expressed below, by the consent and confirmation of the three assembled estates, certain persons were elected to hold the said parliament, and licence was given to the others to leave, on account of the importunity and dearth of the season.

A.P.S., i, 506 (from the ' Black Book ')

1369/70. Since the said parliament had been called chiefly upon several points of the state of the kingdom and the king and the manner of his living and other matters which concern common justice, as will appear from what follows, and since it is not, neither would it be expedient that the whole community should pay attention to a discussion of this kind or even wait upon it, certain persons were elected by the general consent and assent of the three estates to discuss and determine those matters which concern common justice viz. falsed dooms, questions and other complaints which ought to be determined by parliament ; and other persons by the same general council [were elected] to treat upon certain special and secret matters of the king and kingdom before they come to the notice of the said general council.

A.P.S., i, 534 (from the original parliament roll)

1371/2.

[*In the Parliament of our lord king held at Scone on 2nd March 1371 with continuation of the following days.*] The bishops, abbots, priors, earls, barons and free tenants who hold of the king in chief having been summoned and called in the manner used and wont, and from each burgh certain burgesses who were summoned for a certain purpose and for a special reason [*ad hoc . . . ex causa*], all having compeared who should, would or could be conveniently there, certain others being absent of whom some were legitimately excused, but others had contumaciously stayed away, as is contained in another register.

Since the said parliament was ordained to be held chiefly on numerous points which concern the state of the kingdom and the king, and on other points touching common justice as will appear below, it is not and would not be expedient that the whole community should give attention to a discussion of this kind or even wait upon it . . . thus in imitation of that order and procedure which were used in the parliament held at Perth in the time of king David of venerable memory,[1] certain persons were elected by the general and unanimous consent and assent of the three assembled estates to discuss and determine those matters which concern common justice, viz. falsed dooms, causes and complaints which ought to be determined by parliament. And others were elected by the consent and assent of the same estates to treat and deliberate upon certain special matters of the king and kingdom before they come to the notice of the general council, the other members being permitted to leave. The names of those elected as aforesaid are written in the other aforesaid register.

A.P.S., i, 547 (from the ' Black Book ')

[1] In 1369/70, p. 185

FIFTEENTH CENTURY PRECEPT, SUMMONING TO PARLIAMENT

James, etc . . . to his sheriff and bailies of E. greeting.
Because we have ordained our Parliament to be held at E.
and to begin on Monday, 16th of June next to come, with
continuation of days, we order and command you that you
summon or cause to summoned publicly all and singular
bishops, abbots, priors, earls, barons and other free holders
of the whole of your bailiary, and from each burgh three
or four of the more sufficient burgesses holding sufficient
commission, to compear before us on the said day and
place in our said Parliament along with the other prelates,
nobles and commissioners of the burghs of our realm who
have assembled there and then for that purpose to treat,
agree, discuss and determine those matters which shall be
treated, agreed, discussed and determined in our said
Parliament for the advantage of our realm and state. And
that you, sheriffs, be there on the said day, having with you
witness of your summons and this brieve, and that in no
manner you neglect this under the penalty which suits this
case.

Given under the testimony of our great seal . . .

A.P.S., i, 104 (from the Bannatyne MS)

Chapter Thirteen

CHURCH AND EDUCATION

The significant developments in the Church and in education in this period hinge on the Great Schism. In 1378, when Urban VI was elected pope at Rome, England was one of the countries supporting him, while Clement VII, at Avignon, was acknowledged by Scotland, France and Spain. Subsequently, Benedict XIII was elected to succeed Clement, and, when France withdrew her support from him in 1409, he took refuge in Aragon, which, with Scotland, continued to adhere to him. After prolonged negotiations, which at first merely produced a third ' pope ' in addition to the two already in existence, the schism was finally healed through the election, by the Council of Constance, of Martin V (1417) and the deposition or abdication of his rivals.

There was an inevitable decline in papal prestige and authority, and serious dislocation of the normal ecclesiastical machinery, one outcome of which was a strengthening of the provincial organisation in Scotland and the elevation of the ' conservator ' to quasi-metropolitan powers. In 1384 we find Bishop Walter Trail of St Andrews receiving from the pope faculties to grant dispensation for marriages within the forbidden degrees and to exercise other powers normally reserved to a legate *a latere*[1] ; two years later he was empowered to hear appeals in order to save the delay and expense of appealing to the pope[2] ; and in 1401 the estates of the realm, by a statute printed below, formally ordained that appeals should be heard within Scotland for the duration of the schism.

Scottish students had long gone to Oxford, where, according to the Melrose Chronicle, John de Balliol, ' a lover of scholars, made, for the sake of God, a house perpetually endowed, at Oxford ; assigning to each of its scholars every week eight pence,

---

[1] *Calendar of Papal Registers*, iv, 250
[2] ibid., 252. In 1388 an appeal was made from the bishop of Moray to Trail, as Conservator (Robertson, *Statuta Ecclesiæ Scoticanæ*, i, li, *note*).

for their common table.' [1]   Provisions made by Devorguilla, Balliol's widow, for the college which bears his name, are printed below.   With the schism, however, access to England, and latterly to France also, became difficult or impossible for the Scots.   This was one motive behind the foundation of the university of St Andrews.   Teaching began in 1410, formal establishment was granted by Bishop Wardlaw in 1411/12, and confirmation came from Scotland's anti-pope, Benedict XIII, in 1413.   There was an additional motive, namely the spread of heresy.   Possibly Scottish scholars had imbibed Wyclif's Lollardy at Oxford ; at any rate, Robert III, at his coronation, undertook to root out heretics, the reformer Resby was burned in 1406, and Albany, the Governor, was praised for his hatred of Lollardy.[2]   The new university represented an orthodox reaction, and masters of arts had to promise to uphold the church ' against the revilings of the Lollards ' (contra insultum Lollardorum).   It is significant, however, that, despite its anti-papal origin, the university took a leading part in Scotland's decision to abandon Benedict and adhere to Martin V.

ACT OF THE ESTATES PROVIDING THAT FOR THE DURATION OF THE SCHISM APPEAL SHALL LIE FROM THE EPISCOPAL COURTS TO THE CONSERVATOR, AND THENCE TO THE PROVINCIAL COUNCIL

21 February 1400/1.

It is statute and ordained that justiciars, sheriffs and other royal ministers are to attend to and answer letters of caption which are directed to them by bishops and their officials and to make due execution thereof according to the manner used of old, notwithstanding whatsoever appeals or reasons alleged or proponed in the contrary.   Wherefore, if any liege of the king shall feel that he has been excommunicated by an unjust process, let him appeal before the expiry of forty days from his judge to the conservator of the clergy, who, with his council, shall be bound to examine the said process and correct it if it be unjust.   And if it seem to

---

[1] E.S., ii, 664   [2] See vol. ii.

him that the said conservator does not do him right and justice, let him appeal from him to the general congregation of the clergy, where, as long as the schism exists in the church, such things are ordained to be discussed and determined. The clergy, like the rest of the king's lieges, give their consent to this ordinance for the duration of the schism.

A.P.S., i, 576 (from the Haddington MS)

Devorguilla's Charter to Balliol College, Oxford

1282.

Dervorgulla of Galloway, Lady of Balliol, to our beloved brother in Christ, Hugh of Hertilpoll and Master William of Menyl : greeting in the Lord everlasting. Desiring with maternal affection to provide for the profit of our sons and scholars sojourning at Oxford, we will, enjoin and command that all things noted below be by them inviolably observed. In honour then of our Lord Jesus Christ, and of His glorious mother Mary, as well as of all saints : First, we will and ordain that our scholars, all and several, be bound on Lord's days, and on the principal feasts, to attend divine office, and also the sermons or preachings on the same feasts and days, unless it happen that any of them be hindered by urgent necessity, or for evident utility. But on other days they shall diligently attend the schools, and apply themselves to study, according to the statutes of the University of Oxford, and according to the order set forth below. We ordain, further, that our scholars be bound to obey our procurators in all things which, by our ordinance, grant and commission, are known to belong to their rule and benefit. Further, we will that our scholars from among themselves elect a Principal, whom all the others shall humbly obey in those matters which touch the office of Principal, according to the statutes and customs amongst them used and approved. Moreover, the foresaid

Principal, after he has been lawfully elected, shall be presented to our procurators ; and he shall not exercise anything of his office until by them under our authority he
has been instituted in the foresaid office. Further, we
ordain that our scholars procure three masses to be solemnly
celebrated every year, for the soul of our beloved husband
lord J. of Balliol, and for the souls of our forefathers, and
of all the faithful departed, as well as for our weal and
safety ; so that the first mass be celebrated in the first
week of the Advent of our Lord, and the second in the
week of Septuagesima Sunday, and the third in the
first week after the octave of Easter, and the said masses
shall be those of the Holy Ghost or the blessed Virgin, or for
the dead, according to the order of the procurators. Also,
every day, as well at dinner as at supper, they shall ask a
blessing before they eat, and after their meal shall say
grace, and they shall specially pray for the soul of our
beloved husband above named, and for the souls of all our
forefathers, as well as of our children deceased ; for the
safety also of us, and of our children and other friends living
as also for our procurators, according to the form anciently
used. And that better provision be made for the support
of the poor, for whose profit we purpose to labour, we will
that the richer in the society of our scholars study to live
so temperately that the poorer be in no wise burdened on
account of heavy expenses. And if it happen that the whole
community of our scholars shall, in their common expenses
in any week, exceed the portion provided for them by us,
we will and strictly enjoin that, for the payment of those
expenses in excess, nothing at all shall be received beyond
one penny a week from those who, according to the dis-
cretion and decree of our procurators, are judged unable
or too poor to make full payment of those expenses, if an
equal portion were to be paid by all the members. We
will, however, that the foresaid rules shall not be extended
to the long vacation, which lasts from the translation of
Saint Thomas the Martyr to the Feast of Saint Luke,
nor yet to those weeks in which occur the feasts of the

Nativity of our Lord, of the Circumcision, of the Epiphany, of Easter and Pentecost, nor in other cases in which our procurators shall have determined that it be omitted. We will also that our procurators make diligent inquiry concerning the foresaid inability of our scholars, and that the scholars themselves go to our procurators with all confidence to make known their poverty. And if it happen that any one or more of our scholars, contrary to this decree, murmur, or, on occasion of this order, provoke the poorer by any word or sign, we will that our scholars be bound, under the oath taken to us, to reveal to our procurators the names of those so murmuring or provoking. And the procurators, having taken sufficient proof on this matter by the authority of these presents, shall, without delay, expel such person or persons, without hope of returning. We ordain, moreover, that our scholars shall speak Latin in common, and that those who habitually do otherwise be rebuked by the Principal ; and if any one, after being twice or thrice rebuked, do not amend, he shall be separated from the common table to eat by himself, and shall be served last of all. And if he remain incorrigible for a week, he shall be expelled by our procurators. We will also that, in each alternate week, among our scholars in their house, a sophism shall be disputed and determined ; and this shall be done in turn, and so that the sophisters oppose and reply, and those who have determined in the schools determine. But if any sophister shall be so advanced that he can deservedly in a short time determine in the schools, he shall then be told by the Principal that he should first determine at home among his fellows. At the end of each disputation, the Principal shall fix the day of the following one, and shall conduct the disputation, and shall restrain babblers, and shall assign a sophism for the next disputation, and appoint opponent, respondent and determiner, that they may be the better able to prepare themselves. In like manner shall it be done each alternate week concerning the Question. We command also our scholars, and firmly enjoin them, to keep with special care the

Portitorium which we have granted to them for the soul of our beloved husband, and that they shall not allow it to be pledged on any pretence, or alienated by any title whatsoever. Let our scholars also have one poor scholar, appointed by our procurators, to whom they shall be bound daily to give the leavings of their table, unless our procurators shall have ordained that it be omitted. Moreover, that all and each of the foresaid rules be inviolably observed by our scholars in the time of whatsoever procurators, we have ratified the present writing with the security of our seal. Given at Botel, on the octaves of the Assumption of the glorious Virgin Mary, in the year of grace one thousand two hundred and eighty-two.

Nat. MSS Scot., ii, No. iv

FOUNDATION OF THE UNIVERSITY OF ST ANDREWS BY BISHOP WARDLAW

1411/12.

Henry, by divine permission Bishop of St Andrews, of our Lord the Pope and of the Apostolic See legate, with full power throughout the kingdom of Scotland specially appointed, to the venerable men, the doctors, masters, bachelors and all scholars dwelling in our city of St Andrews, present and to come, greeting, with the divine blessing ;— While we diligently consider, and with earnest meditation reflect, that by the schools of letters, through the favour of Him from whom every good and every perfect gift flows, men are rendered learned in the sciences, by whom the truth of the Scriptures is expounded, the ignorant are instructed, the more advanced rise to higher attainments, and the Catholic faith, by an impregnable wall of doctors and masters, by whom thus surrounded she is enabled to withstand heresies and errors, grows strong, it becomes us to assent with kindly compliance to your wishes in these matters, whereby your University—instituted and founded in fact by us, saving however the authority of the Apostolic

See, and by you under favour of the divine clemency now laudably commenced, and which also, of and with the consent of our chapter of St Andrews, we over and above, by the tenor of these presents, institute and found,—and our city above named may flourish together, and the power of the University render the city powerful ; and this, as regards the said University, under the directing influence of anxious consideration, we desire with all our might to follow out, so that it may rejoice in the fulness of its peaceful and prosperous estate, and that the study of divine and human law, of medicine, and of the liberal arts or faculties may be ardently carried on. And that the said University may be rich in the honour of its students we take our foresaid University and you all present and to come, whom we honour with the privilege of our peculiar love, under the perpetual protection of ourselves and our successors, in virtue of the regality of our church of St Andrews, and under our special maintenance, by these presents, and the said University and you all freely we invest and by the privilege of the present writing protect, with the immunities and privileges and liberties underwritten for us and our successors for ever, and these we grant to you and by the tenor of the presents confirm : In the first place, that you have free power of buying (and selling your own goods which you do not bring for the purposes of trade) in our said city and everywhere throughout our regality and our other lands and harbours, all and sundry things whatsoever required by you, and especially those things which pertain to food and diet and clothing, when and where you or any of you please, without exactions of customs, or licence asked from any one whatever. We will also that the assize of bread and ale and appraisings of all things which pertain to food, duly according to the laws and customs of the burghs, be very fully observed to you, and that delinquents in these matters be punished with due correction, and we grant for ourselves and our successors that such delinquents, if any there be, shall be reported to the alderman or any of the bailies by the Rector of your

University, who may demand of the said alderman or any of the bailies, in presence of witnesses, that they be sufficiently corrected and punished ; and if within a natural day the foresaid alderman, or any of the bailies, called on to perform this duty, shall not cause the defaults and delinquents to be duly reformed, then the correction of the same according to the laws of the city, as often as it shall happen, shall be transferred to your said Rector. And if any dispute about such correction and punishment arise between your Rector and the alderman or any of the bailies, we will that the cognizance and determination thereof belong to us and our successors. And if it happen that the said alderman or any of the bailies be by us found culpable or negligent in such correction and punishment, and otherwise in the administration of justice, both the said alderman or any of the bailies, as well as such delinquents, we, for ourselves and our successors, promise to remit to your said Rector to be duly punished, saving the privileges, liberties and customs of the lord Prior, the chapter and Archdeacon of St Andrews, in their baronies within our city. We also grant to the said Rector jurisdiction, correction and punishment on those injuring you or offending against you, whether they be cleric or lay, provided it amount not to heinous injury. We will also and grant that all civil causes, actions and complaints of scholars against any whomsoever, as well of our city as of the regality and our other lands, shall at the will of the said scholars be heard in presence of your Rector, and by him, proceeding summarily and immediately, decided according to the requirement of law. Moreover we grant to you that you shall not be bound to compear against your will before any judge ecclesiastical or secular other than your foresaid Rector, regarding any contracts or civil questions, but in this case each of you shall have the option of litigating before any ecclesiastical judge whom he may prefer. Moreover we grant to you that inns and houses of our city be let to you according to the taxing of yourselves and the citizens to be elected in equal number and sworn for this purpose, and from these you shall not be removed so long as you duly pay the rent and conduct yourselves well in the same, and saving the other cases in the law expressed. To this we add that those beneficed persons of our diocese, actually regenting, studying or who wish to study, provided however they be teachable, having sought leave of us and our successors, although they have not obtained it, may not be compelled to reside personally in their benefices, provided, however, they cause the same to be decently served in divine things during the time of their absence, and that in the meantime they may reap and enjoy the fruits of their said benefices. Moreover, by the tenor of the presents, we will that your esquire-beadles, servants and attendants, as also your writers, stationers and parchment-makers, and your and their wives, children and maids shall enjoy all the privileges above and underwritten. Moreover we shall take care, and we for ourselves and our successors promise, to provide that the alderman, bailies and other officials of our city aforesaid shall, each year on their entering upon office, swear, in the hands of your Rector, faithfully to observe and to the extent of their power cause to be observed all and sundry privileges and liberties of your University aforesaid, granted and to be granted by us and our successors, as far as they are concerned, as well as the statutes and customs of your said University. Moreover, for ourselves and our successors, we promise that we will in no way claim or seek any part of the goods of scholars dying testate or intestate, by reason of any custom or of the production of their wills for registry, but according to what the laws prescribe, the style of latter wills shall be free to every one, and that everything regarding their testaments shall proceed gratuitously and without any expense of legal process. We exempt you also and make you free from payment of all tributes, gifts, exactions, vexations, capitations, watchings, wardings, levies, burdens, and servitudes of carriage, great or small, in our city on any pretence whatsoever. In faith and testimony of all and sundry the premises, we have commanded our present letters, or present public instrument, to be subscribed and published by the notaries public underwritten, and have caused it to be ratified by the affixing of our seal along with the common seal of our chapter. And we James, by divine permission, Prior of St Andrews, and the convent of the same place, along with the two Archdeacons of St Andrews and Lothian chapterly convened, to the institution and foundation of the foresaid University and the grant of the privileges aforesaid by the tenor of the presents give our consent and assent. And further we James, Prior abovenamed, along with our convent, and we Thomas Steward, Archdeacon of St Andrews aforesaid, will that the assize of bread and ale and appraisements of all things which pertain to food may be very fully observed to you, in our baronies within the said city, duly according to the laws and customs of the burghs, and that delinquents in these things be punished with due correction, and grant for ourselves and our successors that such delinquents, if any there be, may be reported to the bailies of our baronies aforesaid by the Rector of your University, who shall demand, in presence of witnesses, that they be sufficiently corrected and punished by the said bailies or any of them. And unless, within a natural day, the said bailies or any of them, who may be called upon to perform this duty, shall cause the defaults and defaulters to be duly reformed, then the correction of the same, according to the laws of the baronies, as often as he shall exact it, shall be transferred to your said Rector. And if any dispute about such correction and punishment arise between your Rector and the said bailies or any of them, we will that the cognizance and determination pertain to us and our successors. And if it happen that the said bailies or any of them be by us found culpable or negligent in such correction and punishment and otherwise in the administration of justice, then we promise, for ourselves and our successors, to hand over the said bailies or bailie herein transgressing to your said Rector to be duly punished. In testimony of all and each these things the common seal of our chapter is appended to these presents.

Given and done at St Andrews in the chapter house of our cathedral church, the penultimate day of the month of February, in the year of our Lord one thousand four hundred and eleven according to the course and reckoning of the Scottish Church, in the fifth indiction, the eighteenth year of the pontificate of the most holy father and lord in Christ, our lord Benedict XIII.

[*Papal confirmation of the above was given by Benedict XIII in a bull dated 28 August 1413.*]

Nat. MSS Scot., ii, No. lxiii

SCOTLAND'S DECISION TO ADHERE TO MARTIN V

1418. In the congregation of the faculty [of Arts at St Andrews] held at St Leonard's on 9 August, it was decided that obedience be withdrawn from Peter de Luna, sometime styled Benedict, and each master of the faculty, with few exceptions, withdrew his obedience and obeyed Martin. They appointed a representative to put the point of view of the faculty before the governor and the three estates of the realm, to induce [them] to withdraw with all formality from Peter de Luna and to declare the obedience of the Scottish Church to our lord Pope Martin V, and decided that their own formal withdrawal should be postponed till the meeting of a general council, out of respect to the governor and the realm at large ; but in the event of the governor's refusal to make the withdrawal, and his continued obedience to Peter de Luna, . . . then the faculty would proceed formally to withdraw.

Acta Rectorum, fo. 4, quoted in Robertson, *Statuta*, i, lxxix, *n.*

1418.

In 1417 was sent to Scotland from the Council of Constance . . . the lord abbot of Pontiniacum, for bringing the Church of Scotland to the obedience of the Council of Constance and for withdrawing it from the allegiance of Benedict XIII,

. . . to whom no province then definitely adhered save Scotland alone. This abbot was considered a most distinguished master in theology, and, in a general council held at Perth, argued the cause of his embassy in a most learned sermon before the governor and the three estates. About the same time, the Emperor Sigismund . . . wrote from Paris to the governor and three estates of the realm to send representatives to bring Scotland into the Council of Constance, as other realms had already done. Meantime, Pope Benedict, as he was then called in his obedience, wrote to the governor and three estates that they should remain firm in their allegiance to him. The governor was strongly in favour of the latter, and appointed a certain English friar, Robert Harding [to promote the cause of Benedict] ; and Harding, in disputations and sermons, put forth many persuasions in favour of Benedict. Against him rose up the whole university of St Andrews. [*After a sermon by Harding to the general council at Perth on 2 or 3 October 1418, the university had his propositions condemned by the Roman court ; but, before the bull of condemnation reached Scotland, Harding was dead.*] And consequently . . . in the same year, the Scots were withdrawn from the support of Benedict and attached to that of Martin.

Scotichronicon, xv, 24, 25

CHAPTER FOURTEEN

SOCIAL AND ECONOMIC CONDITIONS

WARFARE

*Stores in Edinburgh Castle, 17 October 1298 ; and of its
provisioning :*

of wheat, 150 quarters ;
of barley, 20 quarters ;
of oats, 30 quarters ;
of beans, 4 quarters ;
of the carcases of oxen, 20 ;
of salt, 20 quarters.

And besides these things it was appointed then by the
king's council that the said castle should be provided with
victuals until the feast of Michaelmas ; and according to
this appointment of the council the things underwritten
were sent from the town of Berwick to the said castle to
increase the stores ; that is to say, by land, upon 100
horses, 75 quarters of barley to make malt, and 1,000 dried
fish, and 10,000 herrings.

Also by land, brought and driven by Sir Simon Frasel,
100 live oxen.

Item, by sea, in the king's barge, which John le Pachere
of Sandwich keeps, and in a little vessel attendant upon the
said barge, 24 quarters of wheat.

Item, of barley and oats to make malt, 125 quarters.

Item, of dried fish, 1,000.

Item, of herring, 10,000.

Item, of Poitou salt, 10 quarters.

Stevenson, Documents, ii, 310–11

List of the Stores in Berwick Castle, handed over to the Constable,
Sir Hugh de Audley, 22 October 1298

. . . Two light hauberks without hoods, three hauberks
of strong iron without hoods, five pair of covertures of iron
and two headpieces of iron, two pair of shoes of iron, six
old targes, one old shield, one targe of boiled leather, one
pair of firepans, four boxes, seven crossbows with winches
with old cords, and four of them are out of order for want
of cords, six crossbows for two feet, one of which wants
two cords and one nut, and seven new ' costes ' varnished
as it appears, etc., eight crossbows for one foot, all in order
excepting four nuts, one ' teller ' with a winch, and one for
one foot, four old bands, one coffer, three vices, one quarter
of canvas, 189 wings of geese for feathering crossbow-bolts.

In the hall, four great tables, two pairs of trestles, one
form, one chess-board.

In the larder, two pitchers of pewter, one basin of
pewter.

In the kitchen, one great caldron, one brass pot of two
gallons, one possnet of half a gallon, two little andirons,
one gridiron, one oven.

In the bakehouse (there are three in the castle), four
leads, one great tub, three frail ones, four pair of handles,
one trough, a barrel for boulting.

In the chapel, a new vestment (and an old one whereof
is wanting a stole and a fanon), of new cloth of silk, a gilt
chalice, a missal, four napkins, a great cross and a small
one, an image of our Lady, a great ' crawe.'

In the forge, three troughs and three anvils, six pair of
pincers, three pair of bellows, two great hammers, one great
anvil and pickaxe, and one little one, four little hammers,
one pickaxe, four chisels, two tongs, one barrel for beating
iron, twelve pair of forges, one handle, two stones for grind-
ing with, one axle of iron for the stones.

In the great tower for the engineer, four tillers bound
with iron, two tillers without iron, six pieces ' a jowes,' a
tiller bound with iron, three posts with windlasses and a

tiller, a hundred pounds of lead in one lump, and another great piece of brass of ten stone.

In the body of the castle four engines fit for service, one of which has two cords to draw it, and each of the others one cord.

On the walls of the castle are three springalds with all their furniture excepting three cords.

In the little chamber beyond the bakehouse four score and fifty arrows, a chain with forty-eight links, and another chain of twenty-one links, one great iron hammer for the box of an engine, five corner-pieces of iron for the springalds, and seven quarters and a half of sea coals. And four score bolts for crossbows for one foot, and iron for the heads of guards for crossbows of one foot, and five hundred bolts for crossbows of two feet, and three hundred bolts for crossbows with winches, four hundred heads for bolts for crossbows with winches, a headpiece of iron, and a green carpet with a border of red, much worn, which belonged to Sir Osbert de Spaldington.

Stevenson, Documents, ii, 322–5

Purveyance of Edinburgh Castle, 1299

Be it remembered that as our lord the king had appointed at York Alexander le Convers, his clerk, to cause purvey victuals and other things necessary for the castle of Stirling at the order and view of Rauf de Kyrkeby, clerk, and three other servants who came to the king at York out of the said castle, the foresaid Alexander had purveyed in the said manner for the said castle the things underwritten and had freighted with them at Berwick-on-Tweed a ship which is called the Godale of Beverley, of which John Fitzwalter is master, to take them by sea as far as the said castle ; the which things are ordered by Sir John de Drokenesford, keeper of the wardrobe of our lord the king, to be sent in the said ship as far as the Maiden Castle, there to be delivered to Sir John de Kyngestoun for the sustenance of the said castle of Edinburgh, that is to say :

2 lasts of herrings, of hard fish 1,000 stock fish, 610 great salt fish, the hundred counted for six score, 4,000 onions, 1 pack of garlick, 10 sheaves of steel, 1 barrel of honey containing 34 gallons, 2 barrels of peas, 2 great cross-bows with winches, 18 smaller cross-bows, 50 bows, 4 great platters of brass for the kitchen, 100 dishes, half a hundred plates, half a hundred saucers, half a hundred cups, 22 stones of hemp, 20 pounds of wax, 10 pounds of cummin, 6 pounds of pepper, 2 pounds of saffron, 2 grindstones for the forge, 3 white horse hides cured, 6 ox hides tanned for slings to the engines, 1 bandre, 18 dozens of bow-strings, 2 pounds of cotton thread for making candles, 200 goose-wings for feathering, a great parcel of pack-thread for cross-bow strings, 200 needles, 3 pounds of white thread and of black, and a great parcel of binding for robes, a dozen of parchment, a pound of ink, 2 empty tuns for putting the said things in and keeping them, four score and six stones of cheese containing 103 cheeses, 20 stones of tallow containing 16 loaves, 240 pairs of shoes of cow-skin in 2 sacks, and the two sacks and 6 ells of canvas rolled between the said bows and spices, 100 empty sacks for unloading the aforesaid things, and many other victuals which are assigned for the said Maiden Castle out of other ships. Written at Berwick aforesaid, the 28th day of December, the year of the reign of our lord the king Edward the twenty-eighth. And two bushels of mustard-seed for making mustard in one sack.

Nat. MSS Scot., ii, No. xi

The Scots on their Military Expeditions [*in the reign of David II*]

The Scots are bold, hardy, and much inured to war. When they make their invasions into England, they march from twenty to four-and-twenty leagues without halting,[1] as well by night as day ; for they are all on horseback, except the camp-followers, who are on foot. The knights and esquires

---

[1] Here, presumably, the league is to be reckoned as about one mile.

are well mounted on large bay horses, the common people on little galloways. They bring no carriages with them on account of the mountains they have to pass in Northumberland ; neither do they carry with them any provisions of bread or wine ; for their habits of sobriety are such, in time of war, that they will live for a long time on flesh half sodden, without bread, and drink the river water without wine. They have, therefore, no occasion for pots or pans ; for they dress the flesh of their cattle in the skins, after they have taken them off ; and, being sure to find plenty of them in the country which they invade, they carry none with them. Under the flaps of his saddle, each man carries a broad plate of metal ; behind the saddle, a little bag of oatmeal ; when they have eaten too much of the sodden flesh, and their stomachs appear weak and empty, they place this plate over the fire, mix with water their oatmeal, and when the plate is heated, they put a little of the paste upon it, and make a thin cake, like a cracknel or biscuit, which they eat to warm their stomachs : it is therefore no wonder that they perform a longer day's march than other soldiers.

Froissart's Chronicle, i, c.17, quoted by Hume Brown in
Early Travellers in Scotland, 8–9

The French in Scotland, 1385

Articles of agreement entered into between Robert II, king of Scotland, and John, earl of Carrick, his eldest son, and other earls and barons of the kingdom of Scotland on the one part, and John de Vienne, admiral of France, and lieutenant of the king of France in the parts of Scotland and England, and other noble and valiant gentlemen of France, on the other part, with regard to the war to be made on their common enemy, the king of England—

[*The Articles include :*]

That in passing to the Marches through the Scottish countryside, no man shall commit robbery or theft or make pillage of horses, harness, food or other possessions without the agreement and will of the owners, under pain of losing his head.

Item, that all persons who, from whatever part, may wish to come to the host with merchandise and victual to sell shall have surety and safe-conduct to come and to go and no man shall take anything from them without payment or satisfaction, under the same pain. Item, that whoever kills a man in the host, he shall be killed for him. And if a valet strikes a gentleman, he shall lose a hand or an ear; and if one gentleman strikes another, he shall be taken incontinent and justice shall be done on him according to the advice of the captains.

Item, if any riot or quarrel arises between any of the French and the Scots, the two sides shall not fight it out between themselves, but those who started the quarrel, on the one side and the other, shall be arrested by the captains who shall administer justice in that matter; and as for any who does not observe this article, if he be a man-at-arms he shall lose his horse and harness, and if he be a valet he shall lose a hand or an ear.

Item, that every Frenchman and Scot shall bear a sign before and behind in the form of a white St Andrew's cross; and if his jack is white or his surcoat white, he shall bear the said white cross on a round or square black piece of cloth.

And if a Scot shall do misprision, wrong or grievance in the company of the French, the captain of that company in which the wrong is done shall take the wrongdoer and hand him over to the Scots captain to whom he belongs and he shall do justice on him; and likewise if a Frenchman does wrong or misprision in the company of the Scots, the captain shall take him and hand him over to the French sieur to whom he belongs, and he shall make amends and do justice.

Item, if any Frenchman or Scot shall unhorse an Englishman, he who takes him from the ground shall have the half of his ransom; but always the fact must first be enquired into and proved.

Item, that no man-at-arms, under pain of losing his horse and harness, and no valet under pain of losing a hand or an ear, shall set fire to a church or kill a woman or a child, or rape a woman.

Item, that a prisoner shall belong to the man who first received his word of render ; and if another takes the prisoner from him by force, his captain shall hand the prisoner back and shall make amends for the wrong ; and if he kills the prisoner he shall pay his reasonable ransom, and he shall be punished according to the decision of the captain.

Item, that all safe-conducts given by the said Admiral shall be observed and honoured, according to their tenor, by the Scots nobles and captains, to whomsoever they may have been given. And also safe-conducts given by the Scots nobles and captains shall be observed and kept by the said Admiral and his men, to whomsoever they may have been given.

A.P.S., i, 554–5 (from the ' Black Book ')

FOURTEENTH-CENTURY CATERING

Purchases for the Marriage of David and Johanna, at Berwick, on Sunday, 17 July 1328

Item, to buying 23 pieces of coloured cloth, and 23 pieces of striped cloth, for the robes of the knights at the wedding at Berwick, £173 9s 2d. And for 20 pieces of cloth for the squires, and 16 pieces for the sergeands, £90. And for 41 surcoats of miniver, £63 10s 6d. And for 24 surcoats of vair, £22, 16s. And for 73 surcoats of strandling, and 7 surcoats of squirrel, and 100 hoods of miniver, £64 5s 6d. And for 100 surcoats of budge, 40 hoods of budge, £17 10s. And for 4,200 ells of canvas, 1,270 ells of linen, 345 ells of napery, 687 ells of towelling, £108 14s 7d. And for 4,360 pounds of almonds, 600 pounds of rice, 40 loaves of sugar, weighing 378 pounds, £53 18s. And for 180 pounds of pepper, 55 pounds of mace, 27 pounds of gelofer, 10 pounds of nutmegs, 5 pounds of grain of Paradise, 3 pounds of cicovalens, £36 5s 2d. And for 2 pounds of spikenard, 8 pounds of colouring for the food, 74 pounds of cinnamon, 55 pounds of galingale, 43 pounds of saffron, 70 pounds of cooking-sugar in barrels, 70 pounds of cummin, 1 bale of ginger weighing 180 pounds, 1 pound of dragées, 204 pounds of sweets, 41 pounds of special sweets,[1] £53, 9s 7d.

And for 13 pieces of wax, weighing two hundred stones, £51 13s 6d. And for twenty casks of wine, £75. And for 1 cask of vinegar, 2 pipes of verjuice, 2 pipes of olive oil, 1 pipe of honey, 2 barrels of mustard, 7 barrels of eels, containing 2,200, two casks of white fish, £24 15s 6d. And for three large cooking pans, seven large ladles, four large copper baking tins, with the necessary chains, and three large gridirons, for all of which [the Chamberlain] must otherwise account, £20 2s. And to Peter the machinist for buying and bringing over these things from Flanders to Scotland, under contract made with him at the rate of two shillings in the pound, £85 11s.

Total of all this, £941 6d.

E.R., i, 119

And for the expenses of Simon of Saltoun, remaining behind at Berwick, to look after the unconsumed food, and for his other labours in relation to the food provided for the wedding, 65s 3½d.

Ibid., i, 217

And for the repair of the wall of the church-yard of Holy Trinity, which was broken down to the ground at the time of the wedding, 13s 4d.

Ibid., i, 218

Provisions for the royal household in 1330

Following are extracts from the account of Adam of Swynburne, clerk of the kitchen of the king's household, rendered at Berwick

---

[1] xlj libris confeccionum de besandis et cedris

on 15 March 1330/31, of his receipts and disbursements from 24 June to 17 February next following :

He charges himself with 258 marts received from the chamberlain, 26 from the sheriff of Ayr, 16 from the sheriff of Forfar and 8 purchased by the clerk of liverance, in all 308.

He charges himself with $192\frac{1}{4}$ carcases by arrears, 308 marts charged above and $68\frac{1}{2}$ purchased according to the rolls of the expenses of the household, in all $528\frac{1}{4}$ (*sic*). Whereof the household disbursements (witness the roll of audit on account) were $523\frac{1}{8}$, and one lost by murrain on the way, making $524\frac{1}{8}$. So he owes $4\frac{1}{8}$ carcases.

He charges himself with 836 sheep received from the chamberlain, 40 purchased by the clerk of liverance (in the rolls of the household expenses), in all 876. Whereof, 60 to Sir Malcolm Fleming at the obsequies of the lord king at Dunfermline, 5 lost by the way on account of a storm and 37 stolen by thieves or devoured by dogs, in all 102. So there remain 794.

He charges himself with 216 carcases of sheep by arrears and the 794 mentioned above, in all 1,010. Whereof, in the household disbursements (witness the roll of audit), $965\frac{1}{2}$. So he owes $44\frac{1}{2}$.

He charges himself with $16\frac{1}{2}$ swine, by arrears of his preceding account, and with 230 purchased by the clerk of liverance . . . in all $246\frac{1}{2}$. Whereof, in the use of the household . . . $226\frac{1}{2}$. So he owes 20.

He charges himself with 9,766 herring, by arrears ; 2 lasts [1] 6,500 from the *prepositi* of Crail ; 1 last from the chamberlain, paid by Roger Phipil ; and 4 lasts 9,170 by purchase in the household rolls ; in all, 9 lasts 5,416. Whereof, in the disbursements of the household . . . 8 lasts 9,516 ; to the chamberlain 6,000, for which he answers ; in all, 9 lasts 5,516. Thus he is superexpended, 100. But he is also charged with 2,080 received from the constable

---

[1] A quantity sometimes, but perhaps not always, equal to 12 barrels

of Clackmannan, omitted in the charge above. And so he owes 1,980 herring.

The ' hard ' or dried fish total 5,437, of which the clerk owes 71, which however are allowed to him on account of putrefaction.

Salmon total 1,525½ ; eels, 1,715 ; moorfowls, 13 dozen and 2 ; white pease, 4 bolls ; olive oil, 1 barrel ; salt, 20 chalders.

E.R., i, 330–3

A charter of hostellage of the abbot of Arbroath

Nicholas, abbot of Arbroath, grants to Richard, son of Cristin, son of Lochlan, all the abbot's lands in the burgh of Stirling, which had been resigned by William, son of John of Drylaw, on account of default of the service due to the abbot therefrom. Richard and his successors are to render to the abbot 4s 6d in money annually, and to find for the abbot of Arbroath for the time and his monks and lay-brethren and their clerks, bailies and attorneys, coming [to Stirling] for the business and suits of the monastery, as often as they shall come, to each according to his rank, with his household—an honourable dwelling, a hall in which they can eat honourably, with tables and trestles and other pertinents, a larder with a butler, a chamber or chambers where they can honourably lie down to rest, a decent kitchen and a stable for their horses, to the number of thirty or less ; they shall also find, on the arrival of the foresaid persons, sufficient fuel, as well in hall as in chamber and kitchen ; white candles of tallow, commonly called candles of ' Peris ' [1] ; bedding ; straw in the hall and chamber, and salt for the tables. But if the abbot, monks, clerks or attorneys foresaid be entertained for more than three nights on end, the said Richard or his heirs shall not be obliged, in that case, to provide fuel and white candles, but shall undertake all the other obligations for the duration of the stay of the foresaid

[1] Paris

persons and their household. Besides, when the messengers or officers of the abbot arrive they are to be admitted to hospitality without gainsaying ; but Richard and his heirs are not responsible for the expenses of their provisions. We will, moreover, that the said Richard and his heirs uplift the ferm due to us from two pieces of land which Thomas Sanfer and William of Kyrcaudi, clerk, hold within our foresaid lands, along with the proportion of service due to us therefrom by reason of hostellage, and answer to us of the same ferm and hostellage, as for the ferms and hostellages due to us for the other lands of ours which they hold of us as is abovewritten. And the said Richard or his heirs shall in no way sell, pledge or alienate or set to ferm to any person the foresaid lands and hostellages, unless with the consent of the foresaid abbot and convent for the time.

Registrum Vetus de Aberbrothoc, No. 321

Wine for Scotland

1374. Licence from Edward III of England to Thomas White of Great Yarmouth to export 20 casks of weak wine of the colour of Gascony to Scotland or Norway to make the best of it.

Calendar of Patent Rolls, 1371–4, 457

Essential domestic utensils [? 14th century]

Following are the utensils to be left by each predecessor to his successor duly and canonically entering the church of Moray, and [the same rule to apply] to all beneficed men throughout that diocese :

Firstly, in the hall he ought to leave a sufficient table with trestles, a basin with a pitcher, a bath-towel and a hand-towel :

Also, in the kitchen a bronze pot, a sufficient plate, a tripod or chain called a ' ketylcrok,' a mortar with a pestle.

In the brewhouse a leaden vat with a cup, called a

' masse fatte,' a trough (*algeam vulgariter le* trowch), a vat, a tub, and a barrel.

And it is to be known that the said utensils are to be apprised according to the value of the benefice.

Register of Moray, No. 284

BURGHS AND TRADE

Robert I's Charter to the Burgh of Aberdeen, 1319

This charter is the first of a series granting to burghs the privilege of paying to the Crown a fixed rent in perpetuity in lieu of all previous separate payments, including burgh mails, profits of justice, escheats, etc., but excluding great customs. Aberdeen's early privilege and the sum demanded—£213 6s 8d—reflect its importance as a trading centre in the fourteenth century. (Edinburgh's privilege followed in 1329, for a rent of £34 3s 4d). The granting of these charters of feu-ferm, which treated the burgh as a unit in matters of payment, simplified royal administration and paved the way for the withdrawal of royal officials from the government of the burgh, leaving the burghs largely free to conduct their own administration.

Robert, by the grace of God king of Scots, to all good men of his whole land, greeting. Know ye that we, with the advice and decision of the good men of our kingdom, have granted and set to feu-ferm, and by our present charter confirmed, to our burgesses and community of our burgh of Aberdeen, our foresaid burgh of Aberdeen and our forest of Stocket with the pertinents ; to be held and had by the foresaid burgesses and community, their heirs and successors, for ever, of us and our heirs in fee and heritage and in free burgage, by all their right meiths and marches, with mills, waters, fishings, petty customs, tolls, courts, weights, measures, and with all other privileges, conveniences, easements, customs, and their just pertinents by law and custom belonging, or which may in future belong, to the set of the said burgh and forest ; paying yearly therefor the said burgesses, their heirs and successors, to us or our heirs, as aforesaid, two hundred and thirteen pounds, six shillings and eightpence sterling only, into our chamber at two terms yearly, namely, half at Whitsunday and the other half at Martinmas, for all other service, exaction, custom or demand. We also will and grant that our said burgesses, their heirs and successors, freely and without any hindrance, in the fields, moors and other places whatsoever of the said forest outwith the wood of the Stocket, hard by the foresaid burgh of Aberdeen, may perform every kind of tillage, erect dwelling-houses and other buildings, dig fuel, and exercise, carry out and regulate other conveniences whatsoever, as they shall think best to arrange : reserving only to ourselves and our heirs the green-growth of the great trees in the foresaid wood, and game likewise, should any such chance to be found in the same forest. We have likewise granted to the same our burgh, the burgesses and community thereof, their heirs and successors, that no justiciar of the forest or any other person of our kingdom, of whatsoever condition or rank he be, shall in any way interfere with or take cognisance of the keeping of the present grant and our infeftment, or of shortcomings therein, save only our chamberlain for the time being ; but so that whosoever shall be lawfully convicted of such shortcomings or of destroying the green wood, or the game in the said forest, shall undergo the punishment of such crime in his own person, and no other : the chief grant, however, and our infeftment remaining in full force strictly and for ever. In witness whereof we have ordered our seal to be appended to the presents. Witnesses : William, bishop of St Andrews, William, bishop of Dunkeld, Bernard, abbot of Arbroath, our chancellor, Thomas Randolph, earl of Moray, lord of Annandale and Man, Robert of Keith, our marischal, Gilbert of Hay, our constable, Alexander Fraser, our chamberlain, knights. At Berwick-on-Tweed, the tenth day of December, in the fourteenth year of our reign.

A.P.S., i, 478 ; *Charters of the Burgh of Aberdeen* [1890], No. viii

Establishment of a staple at Middelburg, 1347

The Low Countries were the largest market for Scottish trade, and to ease the conduct of commerce Scottish merchants were eager to negotiate for special privileges in at least one town abroad which could thus become their staple port. The incentive to this arrangement with Middelburg, in the North, is probably to be found in the unfriendly relations at the time between Scotland and Flanders. On the same day as the confirmation of the Middelburg staple, King David, writing to his chamberlain, sheriffs, *prepositi* and bailies, relates that Scottish merchants and their goods have been banished from Flanders, and therefore imposes a ban in Scotland on Flemish merchants and all Flemings except sailors, to endure as long as the ban remains in operation in Flanders.[1]

The privileges granted and agreements made between the Scottish burgesses and the merchants of Middelburg are not stated in David's confirmation, but they would enable the Scottish burgesses in Middelburg to supervise and control Scottish trade abroad and would make provision for settling commercial disputes involving Scots. Supervision of the staple later pertained to the official organ of Scottish commercial interests—the Convention of Royal Burghs, which in due course gained the right to appoint the Conservator of the Scottish staple. At this time the organisation is uncertain, but it probably fell within the sphere of the Court of Four Burghs.[2] In the fifteenth century the staple was for a time at Bruges; eventually it settled at Veere.

David, by the grace of God king of Scots, to all to whose notice the present letters shall come, greeting in the Lord everlasting. Since it has been agreed and decided by our council held at Dundee on 12 November 1347 that the burgesses and merchants of our realm should have a staple of merchandise and a mayor at Middelburg in Zealand, as the burgesses and merchants of our realm on one part and the burgesses and merchants of Middelburg on the other may be best able, for the sake of transacting

---

[1] *A.P.S.*, i, 515
[2] See Rooseboom, *The Scottish Staple in the Netherlands*; Davidson and Gray, *The Scottish Staple at Veere*

business, to agree unanimously, which agreement or contract to be made, composed or confirmed between [these
parties] we are willing to hold in all things reasonable and
enduring, and the said concord or contract in all things
as aforesaid we approve, ratify and for us and ours confirm;
and this to all whom it concerns we make known by the
presents :

Wherefore we charge and command all and sundry our
officers and subjects that they presume not to contravene
the deliverance of our said council, under the pain effeiring
thereto. In witness whereof we have caused to be made
these our letters patent, to endure for a whole year from
Easter next. At Dundee, 12 November in the nineteenth
year of our reign.

A.P.S., i, 514–15 (from the original document)

The Court of the Four Burghs

The earliest evidence for the Court of the Four Burghs is in
1292, when the four burghs were consulted by Edward I's judges
about a legal decision involving burgh customs. The 'Four
Burghs' were then Edinburgh, Berwick, Roxburgh and Stirling.
Later evidence shows that the court continued to be prominent
in matters connected with burgh law and its administration, so
that it was sometimes called the 'Parliament of the Four Burghs.'
The last known reference to the Court of the Four Burghs under
that name occurs in 1507, but the name was probably dying out
following the act of 1487 (*A.P.S.*, ii, 179, c. 17), which ordained
commissaries of all burghs, both North and South, to convene
together once in the year to treat upon the welfare of merchants
and the common profit of the burghs. This probably marks the
beginning of an assembly which eventually developed into the
Convention of Royal Burghs.

1369. It was ordained and statute by the said three estates
assembled and elected that since our English enemies hold
the towns of Berwick and Roxburgh, which are and ought
to be two of the four burghs which from of old have to
constitute a court for the Chamberlain once a year at

Haddington, about any dooms which may anywhere be falsed before the Chamberlain in his ayres, therefore the burghs of Lanark and Linlithgow shall be accepted for the foregoing purpose, and from now have been warned to compear at the court and serve it in the meantime.

A.P.S., i, 507 (from the ' Black Book ')

1405. In the Court of the Four Burghs held at Stirling the twelfth day of the month of October 1405, it is decreed that two or three sufficient men from each of the king's burghs to the south of the water of Spey, bearing with them their commission, shall be present each year at the said Parliament of the Four Burghs, wherever it may be held, to treat, ordain and determine upon all things touching the utility of the common weal of all the burghs of our said lord the king, their liberties and their Court.

A.P.S., i, 703 (from Skene's collection)

[This is an unofficial statement of doubtful authority ; but if to be accepted it indicates the gradual extension of membership of the Court to include more than representatives of the Four Burghs.]

David II's general charter to the burghs 28 March 1364

If the burghs were to be able to contribute their share to the payment of David II's ransom, which, with the rejection of the proposals of 1363/4, had to continue to be paid (*supra*, p. 151), then it was essential to safeguard their privileges so that they could flourish by trade and make sufficient trading profit to be able to pay (cf. *supra*, p. 163). In this charter to all the burghs David II confirms their privileges and safeguards them against encroachment.

David, by the grace of God king of Scots, to all upright men of his land, churchmen and laymen, greeting : know that we, with [consent of our] council, have granted to our beloved Scottish burgesses free leave to buy and sell everywhere within the liberties of their own burghs, but forbidding any of them to buy or sell within the bounds of the liberty of another [burgh] without licence. Also we forbid any bishop, prior or other churchman, any earl, baron or other lay man, whatsoever may be his rank, to buy or sell wool, skins, hides or other merchandise under any pretext, save only from [or to] the merchants of the burghs within whose liberties they live ; and so that the merchants may buy, we order them to expose, and to offer to the merchants, effectually and without guile, all such merchandise at the market-place and cross of the burgh, and to pay there the king's customs. Also we forbid any foreign merchants, coming with ships and merchandise, to sell any kind of merchandise except to the merchants of our burghs, or to buy anything except through the hands of the merchants of the burghs, under pain of our royal unlaw. And we confirm by the tenor of this our present charter that these privileges, liberties and constitutions shall endure for all time.

Records of the Convention of Royal Burghs, i, 538–41

Scottish Money

The value of the Scottish coinage declined consistently from the middle of the thirteenth century. The rate of decline was not at first much greater than that in England, but the impoverishment as a result of war and the straining of the country's bullion resources to pay David II's ransom accelerated the debasement of the coinage, although the full results were not apparent until the following century.

From the Assize of King David of Weights and Measures [1]

The pund in King Davidis dayis weyit xxv schillingis. Now the pund aw to wey in silver xxvi schillingis and iii sterling peniis and that for the mynoratioun of the peny that is in the tym now.

A.P.S., i, 673 (from the Advocates' Library MS)

[1] This is a thirteenth-century compilation.

1363. *The Scottish Parliament ordains* . . .

that all foreign merchants, whatever their origin, shall be peaceably admitted to buy and sell as has been the lawful custom elsewhere and that all good money of the king of England, gold or silver, shall be received through the realm of Scotland at the true value as can be given in England.

A.P.S., i, 492 (from the ' Black Book ')

King David II to his Monetarius

1367. Since on account of the scarcity of silver money at present in our realm it was ordained in the manner following by the three estates in our Parliament held at Scone on 27th September last past, with regard to the making of money, that the pound of silver shall be decreased in weight by ten pennies of weight, i.e. that from the pound weight there shall now be made 29 shillings and four numbered pennies from which 7 pennies shall be taken for our use and the keeper of the money shall have one penny for his work and the Master of the Mint for himself, his workers and all his tasks and expenses shall take 11 pennies and having so taken there shall remain for the merchant from the pound weight 27 shillings and 9 pennies. We wish therefore that according to the said ordinance, you coin money in this manner until we discuss it with our council to ordain otherwise. And we firmly command you and order you that the money to be so made shall be of as good and pure metal as the money now made in the kingdom of England or as that which was last ordained to be made in our realm before this present ordinance.

A.P.S., i, 502 (from the ' Black Book ')

1373. Letter of Edward III, dated 12 January 1372/3, orders the sheriffs of all the English counties and of many towns to make weekly proclamation up to Annunciation Day (25 March) against gold or silver Scottish money being taken in payment ; those having such money to exchange it for bullion ; any found after that day to be arrested, as forfeited to the King.

Cal. Close Rolls, 1369–74, 482

MEASUREMENTS

Of the ell.

The eln aw to conteyn in lenth xxxvii Inch met with the thowmys of iii men that is to say a mekill man and of a man of messurabill statur and of a lytill man bot be the thoume of a medilkinman it aw to stand or ellis efter the lenth of iii bear cornys gud and chosyn but tayllis. The thoum aw to be messurit at the rut of the nayll.

A.P.S., i, 673 (from the Advocates' Library MS)

PRINTED IN GREAT BRITAIN AT
THE PRESS OF THE PUBLISHERS